NEGOTIATING WITH TOUGH CUSTOMERS

NEGOTIATING

WITH

TOUGH

CUSTOMERS

Never Take "No!" for a Final
Answer and Other Tractics to
Win at the Bargaining Table

STEVE REILLY

CAREER
PRESS

NEGOTIATING WITH TOUGH CUSTOMERS
EDITED BY ROGER SHEETY
TYPESET BY KRISTIN GOBLE/PERFECTYPE
Cover design by Rob Johnson/Toprotype
Printed in the U.S.A.

To order this title, please call toll-free 1-800-CAREER-1 (NJ and Canada: 201-848-0310) to order using VISA or MasterCard, or for further information on books from Career Press.

The Career Press, Inc.
12 Parish Drive
Wayne, NJ 07470
www.careerpress.com

Library of Congress Cataloging-in-Publication Data

Names: Reilly, Steve (Business consultant), author.
Title: Negotiating with tough customers : never take "no" for a final answer
 and other tactics to win at the bargaining table / by Steve Reilly.
Description: Wayne, NJ : Career Press, [2016] | Includes index.
Identifiers: LCCN 2016010609 (print) | LCCN 2016017447 (ebook) | ISBN
 9781632650481 (print) | ISBN 9781632659507 (ebook)
Subjects: LCSH: Negotiation in business. | Negotiation.
Classification: LCC HD58.6 .R454 2016 (print) | LCC HD58.6 (ebook) |
DDC
 658.4/052--dc23

LC record available at https://lccn.loc.gov/2016010609

ACKNOWLEDGMENTS

'd like to thank a few special people for providing me the opportunity to refine the concepts contained in this book. First to my business partners, Steve Johnson and Mike Crosby: Steve for his friendship and attention to detail, and Mike for having enough faith in my abilities to put me in front of his clients time after time.

In addition, this book would not be possible without the help of Rosalie Puleo, Jennifer Sawyer, Peter Boyd, and others too numerous to count.

And one last thanks to Cynthia Heidelberg (Sydney Harbor), whose friendship, instincts, and gentle arguments made this a better book and me a better person.

We love you, Sydney!

CONTENTS

INTRODUCTION: ENOUGH OF THE WIN-WIN ALREADY

The fifth-most-successful *business* book of all time and number-one *negotiation* book by a large, large margin is *Getting to Yes, Negotiating Agreement Without Giving In* by William Ury and Roger Fisher, published in 1981. The book initiated an extraordinary shift in corporate America's negotiation philosophy from zero-sum to win-win. What was once considered an adversarial, often-contentious struggle between buyers and sellers shifted to a collaborative, problem-solving mindset as it became clear that the zero-sum negotiating philosophy of "I win only if you lose" did not always fit in a world of business interdependencies and cooperation. The authors recognized that, although zero-sum negotiators may achieve short-term financial goals, their heavy-handed tactics often damage longer-term, more valuable relationships.

For more than 15 years, I was a Master Certified Instructor for the Negotiating to Yes Seminar (NTY) based on William Ury and Roger Fisher's best-selling book. During that time span, I facilitated the NTY workshop in almost every industry, country, and business situation to groups of manufacturing line supervisors, sales teams, contract administrators, executives, and others. I also presented the *Getting to Yes* concepts at executive conferences, sales meetings, and corporate retreats.

The Negotiating to Yes workshop consists of two days of classroom lectures, role-plays, negotiation situations, and a proprietary negotiation planner. At the time, corporate training departments and sales managers selected the NTY program with the intention of improving the negotiation skills of their people (mostly salespeople) who attended the workshop. The average cost of the workshop was more than $15,000 per session and non-negotiable. (It always struck me as ironic that the most popular program used to teach the art of negotiating was offered by people who refused to negotiate.)

With time, I became more and more curious as to whether the substantial amounts of money companies shelled out for the NTY program actually translated into better deals and better skills. My suspicions were fueled by the fact that, through the years, my seminar participants raised the same questions again and again, questions to which I thought we had only partial answers.

Smart Questions, Stupid Answers

After comparing notes with the other NTY instructors, it became apparent that there were common concerns and challenges that came up in almost every workshop regardless of the industry or situation. Simple questions like "What number do you start with?" or "When and how much do you concede on the first counteroffer?" and "How do you respond to a request for your best and final offer?" were never satisfactorily addressed in the workshop or in the *Getting to Yes* book for that matter. In response to this, the seminar designers equipped us with a set of "canned" answers as ammunition to fend off the workshop participants who "just didn't get it."

The most common question we encountered was "What if the customer doesn't want to play win-win?" to which we were taught to cavalierly answer, "Well, then maybe you should find a customer who will." When asked "What should be my first offer?" our condescending canned response was "Win-win isn't about offers and counteroffers. It's about relationships and shared interests."

In fact, none of these questions and terms appear in this and many other books written by experts on the subject. The word "counteroffer" isn't even mentioned in the first edition of *Getting to Yes*.

With time, I began to suspect that our proprietary canned answers never sufficiently addressed the real challenges salespeople face every day. Having made my living in sales since my graduate school days, I knew that most salespeople have to deal with questions like these on a daily basis from customers who refuse to play anything except hardball when negotiating. Selling can be an unforgiving business with sometimes unforgiving customers.

So in response to my suspicions about our standard NTY answers, I decided to dig deeper into the world of negotiation, investing a substantial amount of my time and energy reading and absorbing all the available information on negotiation approaches. With so many books and so many competing theories on this subject, I had a good deal of material to absorb. I spent much time and energy searching for better alternatives to the NTY approach.

They weren't any.

The real surprise from my research was that none of the currently available negotiation books answered the most basic negotiation questions. Just as with the *Getting to Yes* approach, my NTY participants' questions were left unaddressed by the most famous and popular negotiation gurus. And as the list of questions grew, the list of answers shrank. All of the books I read answered some of the questions and some of them answered none at all.

Wake-Up Call

Then a client, the largest private health insurer in America, asked for help negotiating yearly contracts with providers of medical services to patients, such as hospitals, physicians, and physician groups.

Almost every year, hospitals and physicians come together to try to hammer out an agreement with health insurance companies on the amounts they will be reimbursed for medical services provided to members of their health plan. In these negotiations, the hospitals and insurers are always far, far apart with seemingly impossible gaps to close. These gaps, sometimes amounting to tens of millions of dollars, needed to be closed in order for the two parties to reach an agreement.

Up until this point in my career, both in sales and as a workshop facilitator, I had never been involved in negotiations that meant so much to both parties. This was like cage fighting. And in addition to the huge gaps between both sides' positions, to make things even more difficult, these high-risk negotiations are almost always conducted in the face of a contract expiration deadline that will leave thousands of people without access to medical care and an insurance company with a potentially fatal hole in its revenue for the next three years. This was negotiating with real consequences and, for me, a huge wake-up call.

Unfortunately, my *Getting to Yes* experience did not prepare me for the no-holds-barred, knockdown, drag-out process of hospital contracting where no one left unscathed and everyone bled at least a bit. As I attempted to apply the *Getting to Yes* methodology to these negotiations, I realized that the popular win-win approach made little difference. The techniques I learned and taught in my NTY workshops had almost no application to the reality of these contentious, high-stakes, and business critical negotiations. Though fine theoretically, the collaborative and cooperative strategy immediately fell apart when encountering a side that played hardball. The idea of win-win was at times given lip service, but in the end it came down to defending your position and giving ground very grudgingly. Most of the tips and techniques espoused by negotiation experts were useless in these complex, high-stakes negotiations.

The people on the other side of this table didn't come prepared to share their interests or cooperate. They came with the intention of getting as much as they could while leaving as little on the table as possible. The most important skill is your ability to take a punch, get up, and punch back.

Surprisingly, in spite of what seemed like impossible odds, 99 out of every 100 negotiations ended up with a mutually *disagreeable* contract of at least one year in length. This was considered success in spite of both parties leaving the negotiation bloodied and exhausted. And it guaranteed that the same down and dirty process would start over perhaps as soon as nine months after the original contract was signed.

In a sort of karmic payback, the same questions posed by my seminar participants were now being used against me as a tactic by hospital administrators and financial officers. The questions I was being asked every day were the exact ones I previously gave "canned" answers provided by the folks from *Getting to Yes.*

These were questions such as "What is your first offer?" and "Is that the best you can do?" And, "Is that your best and final offer?"

The difference was that, now, my answers had real consequences.

Medical contract negotiations typically have hundreds, even thousands, of items "in play," and making a concession in one area meant having to make up for it in another. This makes them one of the most complicated negotiation situations anyone in any business will ever encounter. Health insurers have entire departments whose only job is to run contract modeling software to figure out whether or not a hospital agreement will cover the anticipated costs during the term of the contract.

I learned more about negotiation in my first year of hospital contract bargaining than I had in my 15 years teaching Ury and Fisher's approach.

Lessons Learned

Although it was intellectually challenging and at times emotionally exhausting, in the end, I learned three very important lessons from my time in that industry—lessons no negotiation program could have possibly taught me.

Lesson One: If you use win-win techniques with hardball negotiators, you will lose.

In spite of the global success of *Getting to Yes*, there have been many complaints (from myself included) that though a win-win strategy is noble in purpose, it becomes increasingly difficult to execute as the stakes rise. A win-win approach does not work in many difficult negotiation situations, and can even hurt you in others. Ury and Fisher's approach works well when both sides are cooperative and share multiple interests, especially when there is a great deal of trust between the negotiating parties. When a negotiator with a cooperative approach encounters another with the same strategy, the outcome is often a win for both.

But being good at win-win negotiation approaches does not prepare you for the challenges of hardball bargaining. In fact, it puts you in the situation where you may lose more than you would have if you knew how to play hardball in return. Being "fluent" solely in win-win negotiating tactics limits you to being successful with others who share the same philosophy. A person who approaches a zero-sum negotiator with a win-win strategy is at a tactical disadvantage and, frankly, will lose.

Unlike the philosophy espoused in *Getting to Yes*, hardball negotiators don't think about interests or relationships; they see salespeople as replaceable, products as commodities, and negotiations as transactions. And they *will* play win-win, but only when they have nothing to lose.

Each day, tough customers put salespeople on the spot by asking them to make crucial pricing decisions. Customers don't give you the time to think about the short- and long-term impact of pricing decision. They just want the best price.

In response to the challenges faced regularly by salespeople in the field, they need a pragmatic, proven strategy to help them hold their ground and achieve better outcomes. Although *Getting to Yes* may be useful when negotiating with a landlord (an example used by Ury in the book) or reaching an agreement on a strategic arms treaty (another Ury example), it makes few connections to the day-to-day business world.

It is surprising (to me at least) that, although not actually a business book, *Getting to Yes* is ubiquitous in the libraries of every business school and on almost every executive bookshelf. Don't get me wrong; I think it is a wonderful book on the benefits of reaching collaborative agreements, if only for the

Ury idea that parties who reach cooperative agreements tend to be more committed to terms and conditions. However, when it comes to holding your ground, especially when up against hardball negotiators, it provides very little guidance.

And though supporters of the win-win approach mostly believe it is possible to break down and break through the other side's antagonistic wall, I think that may be a bit naïve, especially in sales.

Zero-Sum or Win-Win

I think of negotiation approaches as being on a continuum from zero-sum (hardball) to win-win (cooperation).

At one end of the negotiation continuum are situations in which you face a tough customer with a hardball, zero-sum negotiation philosophy. Situations like

Zero-Sum to Win-Win Negotiating Approaches

Zero-Sum Approach	Win-Win Approach
Dig into Positions	Share Interests
Distrust	Trust
Fixed Pie	Expanding the Pot
Competitive	Collaborative
Transactional	Relationship

this are unavoidable in the sales world, and it can be uncomfortable and challenging for some. This zero-sum approach is characterized by customers who see a negotiation as something to "win" at the expense of the other side. They assume that there is a fixed amount that can only be divided and the skills of compromise and cooperation are mostly useless. Typically, these tough customers are reluctant to share their interests or show their cards unless they absolutely have to. They almost always believe they have the upper hand, whether they do or not.

On the other end of the spectrum are the win-win negotiators who focus primarily on preserving the relationship and sharing the pot. Both sides typically trust each other and are open to brainstorming and creativity in the hopes to expand the pie and find a solution that satisfies as many interests of both sides as possible. Typically, maintaining the relationship takes precedence over the end result.

Now, you and I could have a substantial discussion about which is better, zero-sum or win-win, but unfortunately neither of us gets to choose. It's the customer who chooses the approach, not the salesperson.

And from my experience, a person who can only play win-win is at a distinct disadvantage. Of course, a negotiator who is only fluent in "hardball" is also at a disadvantage, but their disadvantage is different. I find it much more difficult for a win-win salesperson to recover the ground lost to a tough customer than it is for a hardball negotiator to move to a more cooperative approach as negotiations progress. They are capable of adapting their approach to the needs of the situation.

Now, most negotiations are not one or the other completely. Negotiators can move along this spectrum as trust is built and lost during the course of the back-and-forth bargaining. But in my experience, the best negotiators are able to play hardball first, win-win second.

As for my own personal approach, I begin my negotiations with the assumption that the other side wants to play win-win. But I also keep my cards close to the vest and protect my interests until I get a feel for how open the other side is to "playing nice." It is much easier for me to move from a cautious, zero-sum approach toward a more collaborative discussion as the intentions of my opponent become clearer through his or her actions.

For instance, in hospital negotiations, one way that hospital financial people attempt to get an edge is by telling my client that their hospital is losing money and therefore needs to maximize their reimbursement for financial reasons. What they don't know is that I can read an annual report better than most and can easily determine whether they are truly profitable or simply hiding profits with capital investments to maintain their "nonprofit" status. In response to the fact that the hospital administrator is embellishing, I advise my client to take a cautious approach until these hospital negotiators build trust in other ways. This may or may not happen, depending on how the negotiation plays out. So starting from a "zero-sum" base helps protect my client's interests.

Personally, I believe that the prevalence of the win-win ideology promoted and taught by negotiation "experts" leaves many negotiators vulnerable to hardball tactics and strategies. In collaborative negotiations, sharing your side's interests is considered fair and even encouraged. But in zero-sum, sharing your interests is considered a weakness and foolish.

Take the situation in which you are negotiating the purchase of a new car. Although the salesperson may act like and actually be a nice person, the dealership itself is interested in getting as much for their inventory as possible, regardless of the damage done to the relationship. (Your new car buying experience is statistically related to the brand of car you choose. It is not, however, statistically related to which dealership you buy your car from.) So it is foolish to share all of your interests with a car dealer.

Does anyone really tell a car dealer the actual amount he or she would like to pay or the actual condition of your trade-in? You can bet that the dealer, regardless of how pleasant the salesperson, will always try to get you to pay more *and* low-ball you on your trade-in. That's just the way it works. (By the way, the most negotiable number when buying a car is the value you are offered for your trade-in. Never, ever take the dealership's first offer.)

In spite of what many negotiation experts tell you, it is not always possible to reach mutually agreeable outcomes. Sometimes one side gets screwed.

So whereas the first lesson is that playing win-win can hurt you, the second lesson is a bit more complicated.

Lesson Two: The most important difference between one negotiation and another is not the item being negotiated.

Most authors of negotiation books and creators of negotiation workshops will tell you, "If you've seen one negotiation, you've seen them all." They argue that all negotiations are the same, and because of that, their particular approach or strategy will work for every situation. This allows them to force-fit their tips and techniques into whichever industry, product/service, or situation they want to sell their book or seminar. I call it a force-fit because they never really quite meet the needs of the particular company or situation.

To prove their point, they use examples from strategic arms talks, labor negotiations, or other non-business situations to try to show similarities between negotiation situations. This helps them make the argument that all negotiations are the same and their techniques are transferrable from industry to industry and situation to situation seem credible. In the end, it helps them sell more books and workshops.

This disconnect between the industry and negotiation strategies is the reason that, despite their claims, many of their negotiation seminars and books fail to improve the negotiation skills of their readers and audience.

Even though I've said that these "experts" are wrong to state that all negotiations are the same, they are wrong for different reasons than you may think.

Every negotiation *is* different from every other. Because of this, you cannot use the same skills in every negotiation situation. But the factor that most differentiates one negotiation from another is not the product or service. It also isn't the negotiation teams or how much is at risk. Neither is it the personality of one side versus the other. Although each of those factors is different for sure, they are not the most important difference.

So here is a point I've never found expressed in any other negotiation book, including *Getting to Yes* (#1-selling negotiation book), *Effective Negotiation* (#2-selling negotiation book), or any other.

The most important factor that differentiates one negotiation from another is complexity. And complexity is defined by the number of interdependent variables "in play." The more items that are "in play" in any negotiation determines which skills will and won't work. There are simple negotiations that may have a single item in play like the final price. When you buy an item from Craigslist or eBay, the most common item in play is the price you pay for the item. In those situations, making one counteroffer and having it accepted or rejected can be the entire negotiation.

But in more complex negotiations, like hospital contracts, which can have hundreds and even thousands of items to negotiate, it takes longer with much more back-and-forth. In less-complex, simple negotiations, quick little tips and techniques will help you get a better deal. But complex negotiations demand a more strategic approach and, therefore, different skills.

Laundry Lists

The alternative to Ury and Fisher's approach was pioneered by Chester Karass (think airline magazines) in his ubiquitous Effective Negotiation Seminars. His seminar is one of the most popular negotiation training public programs offered today.

The Karass Seminar primarily provides salespeople with a list of tips and techniques useful for bargaining with customers. Karass's approach, like many others, is a list of techniques that can be used independently from one another as needed. These "tips" can help negotiators reach satisfactory outcomes in simple negotiations, like for a car, a discount on a cell phone bill, and at a flea market. These "laundry lists" as I call them, are useful when negotiating simple, fairly basic, single-issue items. But these approaches are made up of an unconnected series of techniques for countering negotiating tricks with quirky names like good-guy/bad-guy and the "nibbler." However, in a complex negotiation with multiple factors, multiple decision-makers, and interdependencies between terms and conditions, only a more sophisticated strategy will result in an agreement that meets your side's interests. Although a "laundry list" of tips can be helpful, it is not a sales methodology.

The simpler the negotiation, the more tactics come into play and, therefore, the more applicable is a list of tips. But, the more complex the negotiation, the more important strategy becomes and the less effective tricks and techniques become. Simple techniques and "tips" in these situations are mostly useless. So a coordinated strategy designed specifically for the needs of salespeople is much more effective and helpful.

Let's compare two situations in which the complexity is very different. When you go to a car dealership to buy a car, there are relatively few items "in play" to be worked out in the negotiation process. Of course, you have the selling price of the car. But there are options you desire (which impact the price), the warranty offered (if negotiable), and perhaps financing (dealer finance, buyer financed, or some other). This is a negotiation that can begin and end in a couple of hours. Relative to the purchase of a complex and expensive piece of machinery, like a mining truck, the deal is simple.

In the heavy construction equipment industry, though, a negotiation over a $20 million Caterpillar mining truck takes much longer because there is more at risk and the process is more complicated. The items "in play" can include price, delivery, service, after-market parts inventory, hourly shop repair fees, financing interest rates and payment plans, in-field emergency service, and backup equipment. And, as you can most likely guess, if you want to get a higher price for a huge dump truck, you might have to give a bit on the service contract to make up for it.

Relative to haggling over a new car purchase, this negotiation is extremely complex.

But what does the difference in complexity mean in regards to negotiation and the different approaches? It means that although a few "tips" or "tricks" might serve you well when bargaining for something fairly straightforward, let's say a new car or an item on Craigslist, they have little value in negotiations that have multiple, independent, and interdependent variables in play.

When you compare both of these examples to a negotiation between a large hospital or health system and commercial health plan like Blue Cross/ Blue Shield or United Healthcare, there are literally thousands of items in play. Commercial health plans use their contract pricing departments to run pricing models to determine how conceding in one particular

How Complexity Impacts Strategy

	Simple Negotiation	Complex Negotiation
Purchase	Car for $20,000	Mining Truck for $20,000,000
Items "in play"	Price, extras, service, financing	Price, options, extras, financing, replacement parts and inventory, service, liability and insurance, interest rates, etc.
Skills needed	Tips and Techniques	Strategy and Tactics
Counteroffers	From one to three or four	As many as needed
Length of negotiation	3 hours	6 months

section of the contract will impact the overall prof-itability of the entire deal. This is negotiation at its most business critical application.

A three-year hospital contract with a health plan can include inpatient and outpatient billing, Medicare reimbursement, Medicaid reimbursement, private insurer, and out-of-network reimbursement rates, with as many as 4,000 items in play. Almost all hos-pital contracts contain "carve-outs" for high-expense procedures like trauma, neonatal care, and sepsis. These "carve-outs" can be reimbursed in a completely different method than routine procedures and often end up being negotiated separately and then included in the final contract, and so, have to be figured into the overall reimbursement totals. (Right about now, some of you are thinking that this is the problem with our healthcare system. And you would be right.)

Strategy vs. Tactics

This brings me to another problem with popular negotiation approaches: They don't scale. Because most of their examples and techniques are applied to single-issue negotiations, it is difficult if not impossible to integrate those same techniques into large, complex negotiations in which large sums of money are at risk and many variables are in play. Negotiating success is, therefore, highly dependent on the application of the correct strategy to the particular phase of a negotiation.

To define terms: Tactics are the techniques you use to implement your negotiation strategy—things like offers and counteroffers, bluffs, brinksmanship, and so on. Strategy is the overarching objective or goal of your negotiation; it could be maintaining the company Average Selling Price (ASP), penetrating the market, or establishing or reinforcing your company and product's brand in the marketplace. In short, tactics are the techniques you use when engaged in the actual back-and-forth of negotiation. Strategy is different, but related.

Strategy is made up of the things you do when you're away from the negotiation table. It is the overarching game plan you must execute to reach a successful outcome. It is the preparation, re-evaluation, and changes that must be made as your opponent responds to your offer and counteroffers.

Here's a simple example of the difference between the two. If a client asks you for an unexpected and possibly costly concession, you may need time to devise a counteroffer that protects you and your company's interests. So you tell them that you will get back to them at some later time. Then you strategize your next move. So tactics are the things you do while at the bargaining table; strategy is done away from the table.

The more complex the negotiation, the more important your strategy becomes; and in complex negotiations, strategy impacts tactics and vice versa. To use a football analogy, if a coach has a strategy of establishing the running game, his (or her) tactics will include a good offensive line with the ability to open up running lanes and, perhaps, tight ends to block on the outside. He will use plays that maximize the team's ground assets.

But if the team falls behind by 21 points early in the game, the coach must revisit the strategy and revise his tactical plan. He will change his players, his plays, and his formations. Unfortunately, I often find negotiators who fall behind and continue to run the ball.

An example of how I use that in the field, when working with my technology clients, is that I often ask them to "sidebar" before answering questions or responding to demands from their customers. It is an effective way to slow down the thought process and determine the best way to respond to the demands, while better serving the interests of their company. (And I am often asked, "How do you know when your team needs to take a sidebar?" To which I reply, "When a member of your team kicks you under the table." Making sure everyone is on the same page is a very good way to hold your ground against aggressive negotiators.)

The more items in play, the more your negotiation techniques need to be scalable. To become a good negotiator, you need negotiation strategy that works for the simplest *and* the most complex situations.

This difference between strategy and tactics critically impacts the skills a salesperson needs to become an expert negotiator. A salesperson whose product is relatively simple with few items in play can become a better negotiator with a few tips and tricks. But a sales organization that has a big-ticket, complex product with many terms and conditions in play needs to understand strategy and tactics, and the interplay between them. So sending a salesperson to a seminar that teaches strategic negotiation skills is largely a waste of time and money if in fact there are few items in play in your negotiations. Just have them read a good book on the subject.

For a salesperson negotiating a product or service that has multiple items in play, a more strategic and deliberate approach is critical to reaching an acceptable deal. Because you can't really separate the two in a complex negotiation, I've integrated both strategy and tactics throughout this book.

Lesson Three: It is not that difficult to become a better negotiator.

Negotiation strategies that rely on complex models and process flow are mostly useless for simple, less complex negotiation situations. Taking two or three days in a classroom filling out negotiation strategy planners and working through binders with a so-called expert, while negotiating used cars or something else not in your industry, is not a well-spent use of your time or your company's money. By using a couple of key principles, strategies, and phrases, anyone can reach better deals even when up against hardball opponents.

It is important to take a deeper look into the dynamics of negotiation, strategies, and tactics in order to improve your negotiation skills. But my emphasis on pragmatic, useful, and easily learned skills will help.

I'm not big on theory and philosophy. I admit that I'd make a terrible counselor. I like when someone—someone experienced and knowledgeable, that is—tells me, "When they say that, you say this . . ." or "When they do that, you do this" (if you know what I mean). It's not very therapeutic, I realize, but it is effective, especially when you need to improve your skills quickly.

My approach in this book is not based on ideas about human nature, high-level theories about nuclear arms talks, or labor union bargaining strategies; nor is it a "laundry list" of tips and techniques. It is a step-by-step negotiation process following the flow of most negotiations from opening bid to contract signing. It is independent of philosophy and based on real-life negotiation challenges facing people, mostly business-people, every day.

This book combines my negotiation experience as a salesperson and sales manager with the insights

I've gained from 20 years of consulting and training with global corporations in the areas of sales, negotiation, and leadership.

My approach was developed at my clients' requests for help dealing with negotiators who play hardball. So the primary purpose of this book is to provide you with a simple, proven process for holding your ground against purchasing agents, procurement officers, buyers, customers, and bosses with whom win-win negotiation tactics are less than effective. *My process works when win-win doesn't.*

You will find this book pragmatic and useful because it is simple. Becoming a better negotiator is not difficult. In fact, if you begin by using the phrase "You're killing me here!" more often, you already are.

If imitation is the sincerest form of flattery, then the authors of *Getting to Yes* must be drowning in it. Since its introduction in 1981, almost all negotiation authors and gurus have copied (or stolen) many of Ury and Fisher's ideas, acronyms, and techniques without retribution or recompense. No negotiation book or workshop available neglects to pay at least lip service to the win-win approach.

So if it sounds as though I have a problem with the win-win negotiation approach, I do. The collaborative, cooperative approach to negotiating has gone too far, and we need to step back and consider other alternatives, alternatives put forth in this book.

This Is Not Negotiating

A number of years ago I had the opportunity to attend an auto dealer convention with Cobalt, one of my software clients whose applications are primarily used in that industry. Cobalt builds and manages auto dealer Websites, driving traffic and business over the Web. In one of the convention meeting rooms, I found myself sitting with a number of automobile finance people. I took the opportunity to ask them something I had always been curious about.

"Which customer gets the best deal from you guys?" I asked.

"What do you mean?" they asked.

"What type of customer walks out of the dealership with the best or one of the best possible deals? Is it the person who researches all possible options on the Internet and comes in with all the data to back him up? Or is it the person who comes in with a make, model, and price, and asks you to match it or he will go somewhere else?"

I was surprised by their response.

"The customers who get the best deal are the ones who come into the dealership unhappy with the price and leave the dealership unhappy with the price. No matter how much of a deal you give them, they are never satisfied."

"Then how do you know whether that's a deliberate strategy or just a person who is by nature never satisfied?" I asked.

"We never know. They never tell us. That would be showing their hand."

"So do these people get better deals because they work you as much as you are working them?"

"Absolutely, but the key point is that they stay in the game. They don't walk away or make unreasonable demands."

So the best negotiators aren't those who have a bunch of tricks up their sleeves or various gambits they can use in certain situations, regardless of what other so-called experts tell you. The best people at making deals are those who stay in the game until they get what they want or at least something they can live with.

But that is one of the problems with the negotiating game: Dealing with an adversarial opponent means putting up with the tricks and hanging in there. The most common tendency is to avoid the back-and-forth entirely by either giving in quickly or walking away to avoid the hassle and the situation because it can be unpleasant. Neither of those situations is actually negotiating.

I see many salespeople cave in just to avoid the back-and-forth. At the same time, I see many walk out of a customer meeting with the complaint that the customer doesn't want to pay the higher price the salesperson offered.

It is understandable that a person would want to avoid the sometimes unpleasant haggling inherent in hardball negotiation, but some don't have a choice. Salespeople find themselves in negotiation situations everyday that have at least some aspects of hardball negotiation. Car dealers talk win-win, but in reality they play to win at the customer's expense. But with just a few simple ideas, a person can begin to handle and even succeed in contentious, difficult negotiation situations.

Negotiating, as stated by the car dealers, is the ability to hang in there when situations get a bit antagonistic, when things get tough. So, developing a thick skin can help with the process. But it isn't always necessary. By using a couple of simple techniques, even a conflict-averse person can get a better deal.

This Is Negotiating

One of the first questions addressed at the beginning of most negotiation books is to define the term *negotiation* before moving into their own proprietary approach. And far be it from me to upend the negotiation establishment status quo.

In my years as an instructor of the Ury and Fisher's negotiation workshop, I was often asked, "Can you define negotiation, please?" Our scripted answer provided by William Ury, the coauthor of *Getting to Yes*, was that "negotiation is back and forth communication when some interests are shared and some interests are opposed."

Now that might be one person's definition, but it is certainly not what I would refer to as a "working definition." In fact, most negotiation authors and experts seem to make things more complicated than they need to be.

My "working definition" is clear and simple.

Negotiation is the middle ground between capitulation and stonewalling; it is the middle ground between giving in or refusing to negotiate. That's it.

A negotiating party must be willing to give and take. If a price is set and non-negotiable, you are not involved in "give and take," but rather in a "take it or

Negotiation Is the Middle Ground Between
Capitulation and Stonewalling

Capitulation	Negotiation	Stonewalling

Capitulation	Negotiation	Stonewalling
Take first offer		Refuse any offer
Avoid conflict	Back-and-forth	Avoid conflict
No back-and-forth	Conflict	No back-and-forth
Not negotiating	Negotiating	Not negotiating
Pay full price		Only take full price

leave it" scenario. You may think you are negotiating, but if the other side won't play, you aren't playing, either. One the other hand, when you give in to the other side without any back-and-forth, you aren't negotiating even if you may think you are.

I believe this is one of the main reasons that so many avoid negotiation in the first place. This "middle ground" is fungible, negotiable, if you will, and many people are uncomfortable not having something solid to work with. Negotiation includes patience and dealing with at least a bit of ambiguity.

And Not Everything Is Negotiable

A number of years ago, I had the opportunity to work with one of the Nike sales teams. The division

I worked with was called Ekins. (Get it? Ekins is Nike spelled backward.) The Ekins salespeople's job is to sell the Nike product line to smaller retailers, usually family-owned chains of three stores or less. One of the toughest parts of their job was communicating the Nike Market Segmentation strategy to the small chains. At that time in this market, the Air Jordan shoe line was very popular and in extremely high demand. But because of Nike's segmentation strategy, the Air Jordan line was only available to the Elite Nike retailers, which included the major sporting good chains and Nike-owned stores.

Now, often the owners of the small sporting goods chain would try to negotiate with the Ekins sales rep to try to get Air Jordan inventory in their stores. This happened frequently as, at the time, Nike was introducing a new version of the Jordan shoe every quarter. So for kids to stay current or "cool" with their peers, they ran out to the stores as soon as the new model was released. (At one point, Nike changed its release date from the first day of the quarter to the first Saturday of each quarter. This was to deal with the complaint from school systems that saw a spike in truancy if the new version was released on a school day.)

Because of this, retailers could count on a jump in sales every quarter from the Air Jordan release—some retailers that is. The small sports equipment chains had no access to the Jordan line and so was SOL. They tried to every trick in the negotiating book, and every technique taught by every negotiation guru, but the simple fact remained that this was "non-negotiable." It was a waste of time and energy. It was just not going to happen. Period.

In order for a negotiation to occur, both sides have to be in the game. If for any reason one side or the other decides to either give in or walk away, the negotiation is over. Like I said, if the other side won't play, then you aren't playing, either. So some things are non-negotiable.

And besides, trying to negotiate everything seems slightly pathological or, at the very least, highly irritating to friends and family.

I think that the negotiation experts who propose that everything is negotiable really mean that many things that we assume are non-negotiable actually are. It is possible to negotiate things that some people take for granted as not. But we will come back to that later in this book. For now, let's stick to the middle ground between capitulating and stonewalling: negotiation.

ONE

Common Mistakes and Crucial Skills

The Two Most Common Negotiation Mistakes

Before we begin to understand how to better deal with tough negotiators, it is crucial to identify the most common mistakes made by negotiators regardless of the industry, product, situation, or salesperson. Trying to take on hardball negotiators without understanding the two most ubiquitous negotiation blunders would be an exercise in futility.

Through my experience working in almost every type of industry, I've been able to identify the two most damaging negotiation mistakes.

Number One Negotiating Mistake: Giving Ground Too Easily

Literally, thousands of sales managers in hundreds of industries have shared this complaint with me. They complain that the number-one problem their salespeople suffer from when negotiating with customers is giving in on price and/or terms much too early in the process. My own field-coaching experience supports their claims, as every week I see salespeople agree to a first offer or position simply to avoid conflict in the hope that the customer won't ask for anything else and close a sale. I see them concede without making the beginnings of an argument that might help their company get a better deal. This is bad enough when involved in a win-win negotiation, but with hardball negotiators it can be disastrous. Once you give in to a zero-sum negotiator and they smell blood, you can bet they will continue to ask for more.

Why do salespeople give in too early? I believe it is because most salespeople have at least a portion of their income based on incentive compensation and, therefore, a quota to achieve. It is natural for them to want to avoid anything that might make the customer unhappy and perhaps lead to the loss of a sale. Having spent most of my life having to close sales to make quota to hold onto my job, this is understandable.

On the flip side, because it is relatively easy to become a better negotiator, this doesn't need to continue. It isn't necessary to become completely comfortable playing hardball when a couple of key tactics will suffice. Giving ground too easily can be a habit that can be broken with a better understanding of the negotiation process and tools to help.

With the information contained in this book, a salesperson should be able to better hold his or her ground regardless of the product or service.

Number Two Negotiating Mistake: Conceding and Getting Nothing in Return

Perhaps because of the overwhelming influence of the win-win philosophy, too often salespeople give away price, term, conditions, and more in hopes of getting the other side to "play nice" and return the favors. Making concessions without a counter-concession in a zero-sum negotiation can be devastating to your desired outcome, as your profitability quickly erodes. Unfortunately, making concessions to a hardball negotiator is like feeding meat to a carnivore hoping it will eventually become a vegetarian.

It isn't going to happen.

When customers make demands for discounts, better terms, or sample products, I see salespeople respond with phrases like, "I'll see what I can do" or "I have to run this by my manager." And these sales-people frequently concede price, terms, and conditions without asking for anything even close to reciprocal value. More than a few sales managers have complained to me that their people are better at negotiating with them than they are at negotiating with their customers.

Many negotiation philosophies preach the idea that making concessions is bad, and I agree up to a point. But trading concessions in order to get something of greater value to you or your company can be a powerful negotiating strategy with more upside benefits than downside risks.

Also, some negotiation experts specialize in teaching people how to respond to eleventh-hour requests for additional concessions. They think that the best approach to responding to customer "nibbles" is to reopen negotiations or to simply walk away. But that is mostly unnecessary if you understand the reason customers make these demands. The reason people encounter so many last-minute requests for these so-called "nibbles" is because they don't teach the other side that to get a concession, they will need to make a concession; that concession comes with a cost. Beginning a negotiation with a reciprocal concession strategy quickly stops this type of petty bargaining ploy.

So if the two most common negotiation mistakes are giving ground too quickly and getting nothing in return, then the two most important skills would be the opposite.

The Most Important Negotiating Skill: Holding Your Ground

You can quickly become a better negotiator if you understand the strategy and tactics necessary to defend your position in any given negotiation. Many people think that the next move once a price is on the table is to make a counteroffer. That is actually not the case. The next step once your price is on the table is to defend that number. Doing this in any negotiation is important, but it becomes an especially critical skill when up against tough bargainers.

Salespeople who are good at holding their ground typically sell value more than price. They ensure that the selling process is complete before they begin negotiations. Those who give ground too easily are often uncomfortable with pushing back on demanding customers. They think that pushing back means risking the sale.

This is simply not true.

Price is related to value, and the strength of your argument regarding the value your product brings to the customer defines how well you hold your ground. A strong value proposition can determine how close you end up to your asking price. Techniques for holding your ground, especially against tough negotiators, are relatively easy to learn, practice, and become good at.

So once you improve your ability to hold your ground, you are in a better negotiating position. But at some point something has to give. This is when the second most important skill comes into play.

The Second Most Important Negotiation Skill: Trading Concessions

If the second most common mistake is making concessions without getting anything in return, then the second most important skill to improve outcomes for yourself and your company is getting comfortable with *trading* concessions and less comfortable with *making* concessions. It is important to realize that conceding is not necessarily a bad tactic as long as you insist on reciprocal concessions from the customer or buyer. It is one way to ensure a more mutually acceptable agreement with better compliance and accountability. If both sides have to give, then the commitment to the outcome by both sides is also greater.

The skill of trading concessions can be easily learned. It is almost a change in a salesperson's mindset that makes offers and counteroffers much easier to identify and succeed.

A negotiation strategy that integrates reciprocal concession-making quickly improves profitability and commitment to contract terms. Unfortunately, in almost every—no, make that every—industry I work in, making concessions seems to be standard operating procedure instead of trading concessions. The customer always gets the better end of the deal than does the salesperson and his or her company.

The Three Phases of Negotiation

Most negotiations go through three distinct phases. In a simple negotiation with few items in play, a person may go through these steps very quickly: offer–counter–deal. You wouldn't want or need a complex strategy model for negotiating something as simple as a used car. However, in a complicated negotiation with multiple parties and multiple interests, all three steps are crucial. The three phases are: First Offer, Counteroffers, and Best and Final Offer. My negotiation strategy and the rest of this book follow the same flow and development of a negotiation through these three phases.

I begin each phase with the higher-level, more complex discussion of strategy. Although this might not be as important for your specific negotiation, the strategy for each phase differs with emphasis on some factors more than others. Then, within each negotiation phase, there are tactics that help you achieve a better, more profitable outcome, especially when up against tough customers. So although your negotiations may not go through each phase, strictly speaking, the tactics used in each will help you regardless of the negotiation situation. Though all of the negotiation strategies may not be applicable to every negotiation you experience, I think you will find value by reading through the phases in their entirety.

The Negotiation Process

Salespeople are good at taking concepts and quickly applying them to their sales process. For that reason, I am providing a quick overview of negotiation's three phases, including the strategy and tactics that most matter. I recommend people read the entire book, but use the following section as a reference to remind you of the salient points in each of the subsequent chapters.

Phase 1: First Offer Strategy

I think the best place for you to start learning how to better hold your ground is at the place negotiations typically start: the First Offer. Until the initial offer in any negotiation is presented, whether it is the asking price or an initial proposal, the true back and forth of negotiation can't proceed. Until that happens, everything else is positioning.

So the distance between your First Offer and your Best and Final Offer is the ground you have to play on—your "field of profit," let's call it, or "wiggle room." The better you hold your ground, the better the deal for you.

If you make a First Offer and the other side takes it immediately without countering, you might have been better off if you took your time and thought about your opening offer; you most likely left some money on the table, agree? The key to defending your number is understanding the value your product brings to the customer and how to communicate that.

Your Field of Profit

	First Offer	Your Asking Price
Negotiation	"Field of Profit"	Wiggle Room
	Best and Final Offer	Your Bottom Line

The first step in your negotiation strategy is to understand the importance of having a strong opening position or First Offer. You need to put the tough customer on the defensive right from the get-go and there are ways to do that. Prepare to engage with a deliberate and thoughtful approach to protect your profitability and challenge the other side's tactics.

First Offer Tactics

#1: Get them to put their number on the table first.

With a very few exceptions, you are always in a better position if the customer makes the First Offer, especially tough customers. It puts you in a better negotiation position if you know how far apart you are prior to revealing your First Offer. You have the advantage and luxury of knowing how far apart you are before the other side knows.

You should never counter a First Offer before you know the gap between what they want and what you want. Making counteroffers without knowing this gap is negotiating in the dark. If you can get them to share their starting price or request, even a ballpark number, you are better off. This gives you the advantage of revisiting your number and deciding if it is too high or too low. The number you begin with often defines where you end up. The more information you have before putting your number on the table, the better your position.

#2: Make them defend their number.

When and if you get them to reveal their number, the next step is to pressure the customer to justify it. The question "How did you come up with that number?" is one I rarely hear in any negotiation. By using this question, you catch tough customers off-guard and communicate that you are a worthy adversary. Challenging them to defend their starting price or First Offer is the first step in weakening their position and strengthening yours. When an opponent, regardless of how difficult a game they play, is asked to defend his or her First Offer, it puts them psychologically on the defensive, especially if their opening position is not that well thought out.

#3: Conditionally put your number on the table.

After uncovering and challenging their number, you can better determine whether your opening price is too high or too low and adjust your strategy accordingly. If the other side has a weak argument for his or her opening position, perhaps you can ask for more or offer less.

At some point, however, you have to provide the other side something to work with. Once you reveal your number, a good negotiator will test it to determine if you have some flexibility: Is your price firm or negotiable? So how *do* you respond to the question "How firm is your price?" The *wrong* answer is "Firm," but so is the answer "Negotiable." But what is the *right* answer?

#4: Defend your number.

No negotiation guru has ever given me a good response to the question "What number do I start with?" They will tell you something like "Every situation is different" or "It's not about who presents the first offer. It's about the level of trust between the two sides."

Give me a break. It *is* about the number and it *is* about who makes the First Offer, especially if you are in sales.

If you can't answer the question "How did you come up with that price?" or "What makes that fair?" then you are the one on the defensive. The first step in defending your number is having a good answer to those questions. You defend your starting point by ensuring you can logically explain how you arrived at your opening position. Confidently communicating why your product or service is worth the difference in price is crucial to holding your ground. A strong defense of your opening price communicates to the other side that you will fight to hold your ground. Defending your ground is the most critical first step in any negotiation.

But once you know the gap between what you want and what the other side wants, something's got to give. Mounting a sturdy defense of your number is crucial to holding your ground. However, when both sides' numbers are on the table, the only way to close the gap is through offers and counteroffers until you reach some mutually agreeable (or mutually disagreeable) midpoint.

Phase 2: Counteroffers Strategy

This negotiation phase may be longer or shorter depending on the amount at stake and number of items in play. As I stated before, there can be one or more counteroffers depending on the situation. As for hospital negotiations, I've seen as many as 30 counteroffers prior to reaching an agreement. In smaller, less-complex negotiations, like buying something from Craigslist, sometimes one counter is enough.

The Counteroffers phase is really the heavy carry of the negotiation process. It is when strategy and tactics are most important to a good outcome, especially when up against a zero-sum negotiator. When to give ground is a crucial decision, but even more important are the decisions regarding how much your side gives up and how much you ask for in return. Improving your skills in this phase will give you much better outcomes and more satisfying agreements for your side.

Your strategy here is to ensure you establish a reciprocal value exchange whenever possible. But even if you cannot always get the exact value that you relinquished, simply ensuring that you *trade* instead of *make* concessions will improve your deals almost immediately.

Give and take is the essence of negotiation. When giving ground, tough negotiators set the expectation that if they are forced to give something up, they will insist on reciprocity. They don't ever "make" concessions; they always "trade" concessions. You should return the favor.

Counteroffers Tactics

#1: Hard sell every concession.

No concession to a tough customer should *ever* be made with the comment "Sure, we can do that," even if you can. Concessions should be hard fought and hard won. Even a small change in your response, from "Sure, we can do that" to "Sure, we can do that, but not at that price," is a start. Nothing is ever "free" or "no problem" when negotiating with a person who plays hardball. Everything is worth something and therefore should be "traded" for something in kind.

#2: Never make a concession without getting one in return.

One of the most common mistakes people make in negotiations is to concede more and more ground without making it contingent on reciprocal concessions. This teaches customers to ask for concessions without the expectation of ever having to give up anything in return. Though it seems to be almost standard in many of the negotiations I witness, it is very easy to change this mindset. If you bring to mind some of the larger negotiations in politics and world affairs, you can see that it is common for both sides to give up things in order to reach an agreement. Why not the same in sales?

And it isn't necessary to trade price for some other concession. You can trade relaxed terms for a standing order or an acceleration of the implementation time line. The more items that are in play, the more complex the trading can become and the more strategic your skills need to be.

Becoming good at trading items will significantly improve the profitability of any deal.

#3: Trade the things that cost you the least and have the most value to the other side.

If you can get a sale at list price and a "free lunch," take the client to lunch. Salespeople often try to get the customer to "bite" by making a larger concession than necessary. Knowing which terms and conditions are most important to protect is critical to maximizing the profitability of your deal. So is knowing the terms and conditions you and your opponent have to trade. Finding out the items that are most valuable to the other side puts you in a position to create counteroffers that provide you leverage.

Getting the most ground with the least amount of giveaway is the key to dealing with a tough customer. Always trade your least costly for their most valued. The idea is to trade concessions of equal or lesser value if you can.

#4: Challenge their counteroffers.

Tough negotiators rarely expect a challenge to their counters. They think that once they make their counteroffer, the other side will simply counter their counter or take the deal on the table. You keep them off balance by challenging them to defend their counters with logic. Asking them "How did you arrive at that counter?" helps you stand your ground and makes it harder for the other side to go on the offensive. Making the other side work for every inch of a deal is key to getting an agreement that "makes sense" for you and your company.

Never agree to a counteroffer until you are sure it is in your best interest. It is always better to challenge the offer on the table before you counter that offer.

The back-and-forth, offer and counteroffer, make up the bulk of the negotiation process. But at some point, one side runs out of room to maneuver: It is time for a final offer.

Phase 3: Best and Final Offer Strategy

At some point, after the requisite give-and-take, neither side has much room left to maneuver. Having run out of room to trade concessions, or perhaps out of sheer exhaustion, one side has to begin the process of bringing the negotiation to a close. The presentation of a Best and Final Offer forces the parties to end the back-and-forth and consider their options.

One of the trickiest parts in the negotiation process is holding onto the ground you've been protecting while trying to close the deal. Tough negotiators will "nibble" at an agreement until you end up with a less-profitable deal than you thought you had. But even as the negotiation nears a conclusion, you can still use techniques to hold onto the ground you've protected.

#1: Evaluate both sides' walk-away options.

Salespeople often think they are always in weak negotiation positions, especially if they are behind in their sales numbers and feel they need the business. There are, however, two sides to this coin. Although you may not have a very powerful alternative if the negotiation breaks down, the same may be true of your opponent. In a situation like this, walk-away options become irrelevant because neither party has a good option other than reaching some sort of agreement regardless of how unpleasant it may be. The key here is that you are only in a weak position if the other side *knows* you have fewer options than them. And even then, there are tactics to improve your position.

The important thing to understand is that a true Best and Final Offer means the party who makes that offer is willing to walk away from the deal.

#2: Be the first to ask for their *Best and Final Offer.*

Though of course you don't ask for a Best and Final Offer at the beginning of a negotiation, it gives you a tactical advantage when you put the other side on the spot to deliver theirs. Asking is much better than being asked. Timing can be everything in a negotiation.

So when is the right time to ask for their Best and Final Offer? Figuring this out takes perception and experience, two things salespeople have quite a lot of. Although simple negotiations can have one or two counters before a Best and Final Offer, determining when to ask for their final offer in a complex negotiation is more an art than a skill.

As offers and counters go back and forth, keep an eye on the degree the gap is closing and the momentum toward an agreement. You will get a feel for it with time.

#3: Always counter their Best and Final Offer.

This may seem contradictory to the previous "rule" until you think about it. This also seems straightforward enough, but is often overlooked as a negotiation tactic. When presented with a Best and Final Offer, always ask for "one more thing" to see if their Final Offer really is final. This is a favorite tactic of tough negotiators. It can be a tricky decision figuring how much you ask for on top of their Final Offer, and perhaps you won't get it. But even if they don't give in, at the very least you will keep them off balance.

#4: Never let them counter your Best and Final Offer.

If you truly offer your Best and Final Offer, never, *ever* make another concession. A true Best and Final Offer means you are willing to let the business go to someone else: You are willing to walk away. To give in and cough up another concession is to weaken your position in this and future negotiations. However, in most industries I encounter parties that are used to delivering multiple Best and Final Offers, which actually negates the definition of the terms. But it is possible to avoid this pitfall with some very basic tactics and phrases.

The balance of this book will provide you with more details, techniques, and tactics for holding your ground. However, the essence of this book can be summed up in one simple recommendation: Get comfortable using the phrase *"You're killing me here!"*

The added benefit of my set of negotiation strategies and tactics is that they will help you reach better agreements in *any* negotiation: zero-sum or win-win.

TWO

The First Offer

Holding Your Ground

The hospital administrator pushed a note typed on official hospital letterhead across the table saying, "Here is our letter of intent to 'term' our agreement. If we don't get what we want, we will let the contract expire and you will be SOL. We don't have to do business with you. You need us more than we need you."

(A term letter is the formal document a hospital uses to communicate to the medical insurance company that the hospital will allow the current contract to expire or term-inate at the end of its contract period. When and if a hospital contract is allowed to "term," the members (patients) must be notified that they will need to make arrangements with other doctors and/or hospital to maintain coverage. In short, it is a threat to the insurer to provide a better deal . . . or else.)

Stupid move, I thought to myself.

The guy was acting tough, hoping to put us on the defensive, but it was obvious that he hadn't thought this not-very-veiled threat completely through. What he didn't realize was that using his "term" letter as a bargaining chip would only work if the hospital was willing to follow through with the threat—and it wasn't. There was too much at risk for his side. Walking away would cost him and his hospital much more than it would cost my client. And if he had to pull that piece of paper back to his side of the table, most of his leverage would be gone.

But he carried on in spite of his amateur ploy.

"So what's your first offer?" he said with a smug smirk.

"We don't know yet. We have some questions we'd like to begin with."

"We don't have time to answer your questions. Just tell us what you want."

"Sorry, but we can't do that until we have some idea of what you and your hospital are looking for in a new contract. There are a lot of considerations and we need to have some more information before we can arrive at a specific number." I held my ground.

"Okay, we are looking for a 15-percent increase over last year," he rashly said, believing he had more leverage than he actually did.

I stopped and thought for a minute.

"If you don't mind me asking, how did you come up with your demand for a 15-percent increase?" I asked politely.

"I do mind you asking. That's what we want and that's that."

"Okay, I can understand that your hospital thinks it needs a 15-percent increase, but why that number? Why not 14 or 16 percent?"

He was getting irritated, which was fine with me.

"It's simple; our hospital is getting crushed by labor costs. Our nursing expenses increased 15 percent from last year, so we need to make that up with your contract. You can do that much math, right?" he said condescendingly.

"I see. But then how much do your nursing expenses make up of your total hospital budget?"

"What does that matter? What do you mean?" His eyes shifted to his colleagues, nervously.

"Well, if your nursing expenses are increasing by 15 percent, but only make up 10 percent of your total costs, then you are asking me to cover a lot more than just nursing costs. A 15-percent increase across the board would be much more revenue than just the increase in your nursing costs. I don't see how that is fair."

"Doesn't matter if it is fair. We just want a 15-percent increase."

"Right. But I can't propose 15 percent unless there is a logical reason."

He was rattled.

"Uh, do you mind if you give me and my colleagues here a couple of minutes? We'd appreciate it."

"Sure, take your time. We'll just wait outside the conference room until you are ready."

They all looked a little sheepish and shaken.

Five minutes stretched to 20 minutes, but finally our team was called back into the conference room by the administrator. He looked a bit hang-dogged with his tail between his legs.

"We had a long conversation and came to a decision." His tone had changed significantly. He was almost contrite.

"We want to come clean and start over again if you will let us."

"Sure, Bill. Not a problem. I am sure we can work something out," I replied. It's always a good idea to let a negotiator save face when they are eating crow.

"So here is our proposal. We really need to increase your payments to us on some of the really expensive procedures. Our costs on trauma, NICU [neonatal intensive care unit], and sepsis cases are killing us. Can you help us out there?"

"I think we can, but if you don't mind, let's look at some areas we might be able to reduce our costs while making you whole on the expensive patient reimbursement," I said.

"Sounds great. Let's dig into the numbers."

From then on the negotiation became more of a discussion than a disagreement. We were able to reach a deal. It wasn't a perfect deal, but a deal.

First Offer Strategy

Before we go on, there is one more crucial point of differentiation between my negotiation method and others. Many, in fact most, negotiation books, seminars, and philosophies separate the skill of negotiating from the skill of selling. They are treated as distinct and separate subjects. This may be because there are certain negotiations like nuclear arms talks, labor relations, and so on that may not overtly use the term *selling*.

In a sales situation, however, selling and negotiation are inseparable. They are critically dependent upon each other and the outcome of one depends on how good you are at the other. You cannot treat them as separate subjects.

The explanation of this concept is as simple as it is critical.

In any negotiation, there are only two ways to narrow the gap between the low price a buyer wants to pay and the higher price a seller wants to charge. Either you convince the buyer that the value of your product or service offsets the difference in price (selling), or you trade concessions until you reach a mutually agreeable or disagreeable compromise (negotiating).

Only Two Ways to Close the Gap

Seller		Buyer
How much you want to charge	The Gap	How much buyer wants to pay
	Convince the buyer that the value is worth the difference ⬅	
	Trade concessions until agreement is reached ➡	

One very good indicator of whether a salesperson typically sells on price and not value is how early he or she puts a price on the table. Once a price is on the table, most negotiations become about how much or how little the customer will end up paying. A more skilled salesperson will often ignore requests for price quotes until he or she has established enough value to justify his or her company's price. Salespeople who reach more successful outcomes are good at selling and negotiating. Salespeople who sell on price routinely reach less profitable agreements, if any at all.

Many if not most salespeople say that customers often demand prices before they let the sales process begin. They argue that their job is often to respond to customers' RFPs (requests for proposal) or make a bid on a competitive proposal. Let's get one thing straight. Responding to an RFP or bidding is not negotiating. If there is no back-and-forth, then neither side is negotiating. These situations make selling before the RFP or proposal even more important. Differentiation takes place during the selling process, not the negotiation process.

This means that salespeople who are good at positioning the value of their products and services put themselves and their companies in better negotiation positions. Those who do a poor job of differentiating their product or service almost always find themselves defending their prices and are at a disadvantage in holding their ground against customers. They make it more difficult on themselves from a negotiating perspective because the first crucial step to defending your position is convincing the other side that your product is valuable—more valuable than your competition.

This is a very important point as we will see.

At some point, in order for any negotiation to begin, one side needs to put a number out there. And sometimes that person is you. So figuring out your opening price is one of the first and most important strategic decisions; some would argue it is the most critical decision.

This question came up over and over again in my win-win negotiation workshops. The participants would often pose the question in a number of ways: "How do you know where to start a negotiation?" or "What number do I start with?" or "What number is fair?"

Our canned responses in sticking with the win-win philosophy were "Don't think price and terms; think win-win" or "It's not about the price; it's about the relationship." And though that may have been good advice in a collaborative negotiation, it was use-less in zero-sum. Some negotiations are about price and some are not about relationships.

So in a sort of noble desperation, I looked for the answer to this question in many negotiation books and articles. I also sought to answer these questions by asking the same to other negotiation "experts." I found myself as frustrated by their answers as my workshop participants were by mine. I became more and more frustrated by the lack of direction and confidence in any of the answers I was given. The most common expert advice was, "It depends." My follow up, "What are the things it depends on?" and the answer, "Even that depends," just fueled my frustration.

Then one day, I happened to be in an especially combative negotiation between a large commod-ity company and its customer over the price of wire cable. My client supplies cable to telecoms, housing, and many other industries. I was interested in seeing how negotiations play out in a market in which the products are highly commoditized when most suppli-ers are aware of the pricing and terms and conditions of their competitors. After all, cable is cable—or so I thought.

My client and his customer were at logger heads over price and I was there to see if I could help work something out.

And I remember this very clearly. At one point in our discussion, my client's customer said in frustration, "Your price is just not competitive. We would love to do business with you, but at this price, I'm not sure it's going to work."

I looked at my client to see how he would respond to this challenge. But his unexpected response gave me the long-sought-after answer in one short and sweet counter-punch.

The sales manager used a beautiful phrase: "Our price is fair and reasonable, and let me tell you why."

Like a curtain opening, the answer came to me in a blast of clarity. The answer to the question wasn't a specific number or a quick counteroffer at a reduced price. It also wasn't a stupid, "It depends."

All of the stupid, obtrusive, and Pollyanna answers I was taught to mindlessly spout were swept away with one simple and clear rule: The price you start with is the price you can defend. It seemed so obvious once I heard it, but I had never run across it in any negotiation book or seminar.

The first step in holding your ground in a negotiation isn't by pushing it off as a decision from upper management you had no control over, or by the contracts that were negotiated without your input. It also isn't making a counteroffer with a lower price.

The most important first negotiation step for any salesperson is to be able to defend the price of their product or service by communicating the value they bring to the customer and his or her stakeholders. It dawned on me that the best defense against price erosion is value, duh.

Let me give you a simple example to illustrate this somewhat theoretical idea.

Suppose you have a car you'd like to sell. Prior to listing it for sale, you determine the Kelley Blue Book (KBB) value for the car is $15,000. Having taken very good care of this particular automobile, you decide to list it for $17,000—$2,000 more than the KBB value.

Next, let's suppose you receive a call from an interested party who says, "I'm interested in your car, but the Kelley Blue Book is only $15,000 and there are other cars like yours on the Web for a lower price."

A poor negotiator responds with, "Well, would you be willing to pay $16,500 for it?"

This is a less-than-optimal response. By conceding too early, this negotiator gave away a substantial amount of profit for no reason. It's called "caving."

The better response would be, "This car is worth $17,000 and let me tell you why . . . ."

The stronger your value proposition, the better your argument, the better you are at holding your ground. How well you defend your price is the most important factor in holding your ground in any negotiation. Having a strong ending to the phrase "Our price is fair and reasonable, and let me tell you why." puts you instantly on the offensive. Value offsets price, but that isn't the only genius in the cable company sales manager's response.

This was one of three lessons I learned from this relatively short negotiation interaction.

Here is the second eye-opening point:

After hearing this story, you might mistakenly think that my cable wire client was able to hold the line and get the customer to pay the originally quoted price. The idea being that if you convince your customer of the value of your product or service, you get what you want. But that was not the case—and not the point. In fact, my client did not walk away with an agreement at the originally quoted price. He still had to provide a discount from his original offer.

The truly crucial point is that my client walked away with an agreement at a better price than he would have if he hadn't made the argument. Pure genius!

Without the ability to communicate clear differentiation points, he would have most likely had to discount even further. This is the reason sales managers are often frustrated by requests from their salespeople for customer discounts. When a customer or a salesperson argues for a price to match a competitor, it is a pretty clear indicator that negotiations began before the selling process was complete. Price becomes an issue early in a negotiation when the customer doesn't see any differentiation between the competition and the product and services you offer.

In the example of your used car, finishing the sentence, "My asking price is $2,000 above Kelly Blue Book because this car is worth it and let me tell you why . . ." doesn't ensure that you will receive your full asking price. But it does ensure that you get more for your car than if you hadn't made that argument. Capice?

Having worked with salespeople around the world in many diverse industries, I can attest that the best salespeople are also the best negotiators. Because they believe in their product or service and the value they bring to their customer, they have a distinct advantage over the salespeople who lead with price. A skilled negotiator makes a good argument for the value of his or her products and services before giving ground, and that is a selling skill. Lesser-skilled salespeople think that the first step in negotiating is to give a concession to see if the other side might bite.

Here is the third revelation I had while watching these two go at it:

My client did not attempt to differentiate their product, cable wire, from that of its competition by talking about the product's features and benefits. I'm not even sure it is possible to differentiate something that is sold by the ton and by the mile. After all, it's just cable, right?

Instead, my client held his ground by explaining how the company provides better post-sales service and in-field support, better response time to emergency orders, better pricing terms and conditions, and other "value added" services. It was an awesome display of differentiation that had nothing to do with the product itself; all the value came from the things the company had put in place to help better service and support its customers.

Salespeople tell me all the time how important relationships are in their businesses. And that is true. It is important to recognize that, in business,

Holding Your Ground

Negotiator	Vendor	The Gap	Customer	Negotiator
What you want	Desired selling price		Desired buying price	What they want
Your strategy	Defending your position		Eroding your position	Their strategy
Your ammunition	Value proposition		Devalue proposition	Their ammunition
Tactical argument	"We are the best"		"You are the worst"	Tactical argument

relationships are important. But something to ponder is that a "relationship" in business is different from a "relationship" in personal life.

Salespeople often think of customer relationships in too narrow of terms. And this narrows their ability to hold their ground.

When you think about it, your customer has a relationship with you, the salesperson. But they also have a relationship with your product, your service and support organization, and your company as a financial entity. So although your company may have a product that is considered, and in fact may be, a commodity, like wire cable, that doesn't necessarily put you into a commoditized negotiation. It is possible that something other than your product can be a competitive differentiator. If you can differentiate one or all of the relationships the customer has with your company, then you can defend your price better.

To be an effective negotiator, you cannot afford to think that your product or company is a commodity. And you cannot afford to buy into attempts by tough customers to "devalue" your product offering, especially because this is an accepted tactic by hardball negotiators. I've been in the position to see the same buyers tell multiple salespeople that their company is "the worst" to deal with. They look for any mistake or problem to use as a leverage tool to get a better price. Tough customers will use a late shipment or a customer service lapse or perhaps even something that might not be true to get a better deal. They feel it is acceptable to use this as a negotiation ploy even though it is impossible for more than one company to be "the worst."

So your job as a negotiator is to build up the value of your product, service, or company. And the job of a tough customer is to minimize or contradict your value-based argument. You talk about your company's value proposition and they complain that your company is hard to do business with. You talk about the impact your product has on productivity and they talk about the lack of post-service support. Essentially, the ability to firmly communicate the value you bring to the customer is crucial to holding your ground.

See it from the point of view of a tough customer. Their job is to counter your value proposition with a devalue proposition. They will use any and all tactics to get you to fold, including embellishment, deception, and flat out lying. You have to stick to your guns by using your value proposition in response to the customer's attempt to devalue your product, service, company, or whatever you use to increase the value to them. Don't let them get away with it; catch them early and often.

I had a sales training company interested in buying the rights to the workshop our company, SPJ Consulting, leads based on the ideas in this book. Again and again, the company CEO used the statement "There are plenty of negotiation workshops we have to choose from." Because I knew that he was positioning by using this negotiation ploy, I felt the need to stop him every time with the statement "With all due respect sir, you are comparing apples to oranges. This workshop is significantly different and better than any and all the others."

In the end, we could not reach an agreement because he continued to lump my approach in with all the other off-the-shelf negotiation seminars. He thought this would give him the advantage of getting a better deal. In fact, it cost him a good deal.

To further illustrate, let's use two people, a buyer and a seller, arguing over the merits of a black, four-door, Ford Taurus automobile with no extras or whistles and bells.

The buyer says, "This is the most basic car anyone could ever buy." (Devalue proposition.)

The seller says, "Yes, they are in pretty high demand." (Value proposition.)

The buyer counters, "But they're everywhere. A dime a dozen." (Devalue proposition.)

The seller counters, "Yes and there is a reason for that: best-selling car of the year." (Value proposition.)

The buyer says, "But it's black, which is the worst color." (Devalue proposition.)

The seller says, "Yes, but black is the most popular color of any automobile. Just look it up." (Value proposition.)

And the buyer says, "But it's the most basic model with no extras." (Devalue proposition.)

To which the seller responds, "But it gives you the ability to add any after-market options. It's totally customizable." (Value proposition.)

This may seem like an unrealistic scenario, but hopefully you can apply the idea to the products and services you sell.

When you think about it, that's the customer's job: to make you and your company into a commodity. Why? Because that gives them leverage. It gives them the upper hand if you, your product, your service and support, and company are just the same as everybody else in the industry.

A negotiator who buys into that is a less-successful negotiator. It is always more difficult to defend your price if you don't defend your product.

The best salespeople/negotiators believe in their products and their company. It is much easier to hold your ground when you truly believe that the product you are selling is worth the difference.

Do the Caterpillar salespeople believe their products are better than Kumatsu? Of course. Do Nike salespeople believe their products are better than Adidas? Of course. Do Pacific Life salespeople believe their products and service are better than MetLife? Of course.

That is why these companies have significantly higher average selling prices than their competitors; because they believe in their products, their companies, and their service and support organizations. No customer can convince them otherwise.

But customers will continue to commoditize and companies will continue to differentiate, because those are the rules of the game.

Going back to my wire cable client, the product is difficult to differentiate because it is very much a commodity. But the company found a way to differentiate in the areas of service, support, and financing. Making that argument and communicating the value of those differentiators allowed my client to get more for its products than its competitors.

You and/or your company have to figure out how to differentiate your product offering. Without a firm and clear definition of the value your product, service, and company bring to a customer, it is tougher to defend your price.

So my cable manufacturer's salespeople can finish the sentence with "Our price is fair and reasonable because we offer better service or better support or better financing or better sales representation." This can be a differentiator and, therefore, translate into a better price for your product than you would have received had you not made the argument.

Some of you may be saying, "Yes, but my product really is a commodity. We don't do a good job of differentiating our products, services, or any other aspect that might add value for our clients. And that is why we don't have any negotiation leverage." To be honest, there are some companies I work with whose offering is "generic." Their offering is the same as their competitors with little ability to differentiate for whatever reasons. So it would seem logical that they have little ammunition to hold their ground in a negotiation. But that's not true.

Keep in mind that there are *two* ways to close the gap between the low price a customer wants to pay and the higher price you want to sell. The first is convincing the other side that the value you, your company, and your product or services bring to the customer is worth more than the competition.

If that is not the case, though, if your product truly is a commodity, you still have another tool to help you reach a profitable agreement: an intelligent strategy for trading concessions. Even if you have a "me too" product, you can still get a better deal by "horse-trading" to reach a mutually agreed upon midpoint you can live with. So the more your product lacks differentiation, the better you have to be at trading concessions.

This concept of using your company value proposition as a tool to help hold your ground is not covered in any other negotiation approach I am aware of, yet it seems so basic and necessary. Perhaps it is the overemphasis on win-win approaches that keep them from having to face this seemingly simple concept.

I immediately put this to work in my own business. The very first tactic I use when asked to quote a price for my workshops is to ask my potential customer if he or she would mind if I first explain how I came up with my price. I ask them if I could take a moment to explain why my services are worth more than my competition and the value I bring to them and to their company. Some are taken off guard, but most agree to let me explain my reasoning.

If you will play along with me, I will share my defense with you.

I first point out that negotiation workshops are a dime a dozen. From Karass (think airline magazine insert) to Ury (*Getting to Yes*), there are many different negotiation "products" out there. Also, most of these companies offer only "off the shelf" seminars with little to no customization to the specific industry of the potential buyer. I then point out that the cost of these "public" (a public program is offered in different cities on different dates anyone can attend) programs are usually between $1,000 and $2,000 per seminar day, not including travel expenses, hotel rooms, and meals per person. The final point I make is that if a company wants to send 20 salespeople (the typical number of participants we limit in our seminars) to one of these seminars, it would most likely cost between $30,000 and $40,000 plus travel expenses.

I can charge them half that amount for a fully customized, client-site workshop with negotiation scenarios specifically designed for the day-to-day challenges their people face in the field with customers. Our value proposition is "We connect corporate profitability strategies to in-field pricing decisions." (I always tell potential customers that our prices are negotiable. I also add that they should be aware that I am rather good at holding my ground and if I give ground, I will ask for something in return. They all smile.)

First Offer Tactics

#1: Get them to put the number on the table first.

The objective of tough negotiators at the beginning of any negotiation is to put you in a defensive position immediately. This gives them the upper hand and helps them build momentum toward an agreement that favors their own agenda. They want you to capitulate and give them what they want without any back-and-forth. Tough customers like it better if you don't negotiate at all. And though opening negotiations with a tough customer can be uncomfortable, remember that this is the impact they desire. If you capitulate or stonewall, you play directly into their hands. One thing to remember is to stick with your game plan and stay calm, regardless of how much of a jerk the other side is being. A thick skin helps, but isn't always necessary. The tactics in this section will quickly subdue the other side's approach and begin to even the playing field, perhaps even giving you the upper hand.

So the strategy for the first phase of negotiation is to disarm them with a strategy of your own—a tried and proven strategy.

Regardless of what you have been told in the past, negotiations don't actually begin until one side proposes an initial price or takes an opening position. Negotiation experts will tell you that the preparation prior to presenting opening offers significantly affects the outcome of your negotiation, and that is true. But in many cases, people, especially salespeople, don't have the luxury of spending hours preparing to negotiate when customers or buyers put them on the spot to give them a price or proposal. And in most routine negotiations, like a car or an item on Craigslist, one party has to give a counteroffer quickly. So the price you start with will often dictate the price you end up at.

One of the initial challenges you will encounter with a tough customer is their desire to put you off balance at the beginning of the negotiation and keep up the pressure. It's called positioning and can be effective if you don't realize it is being used against you. Tough customers will intentionally use positioning statements to throw you off.

I hear variations of the same positioning statements at the beginning of clients' negotiations every week. Statements like "You need us more than we need you" or "You do want our business, don't you?" or "We gave you a lot of business last year so we are going to want some significant reductions in price" are intended to soften you up for the bargaining that follows.

In order to even the playing field, it is important to identify and deal with these positioning statements immediately. When a customer says, "You need us more than we need you," you respond with something like "Actually, 'need' is too strong a word. We'd rather reach a mutually acceptable agreement." When the customer says, "You *do* want our business, don't you?" your response is "We want any business that makes sense for our company." And finally, "We gave you a lot of business last year" should be deflected with "We are very happy to have had you as a customer last year, but we actually feel as though we delivered very good value for the money you spent with us."

This may seem petty, but when you realize how petty a game the other side is playing, it is fair game. When customers attempt to position, your job is to counter-position, especially prior to beginning to discuss price.

So whereas *their* objective is to push you off-balance and get you to capitulate, your objective is to counter-position and hold your ground from any and all challenges. Tough customers measure success by how close they end up to their opening price; you should do the same.

The first step in building a strong negotiation position is getting the other side to make the first offer; you are almost always in a better position if the other side puts their number out there before you do, especially with hardball negotiators. Savvy negotiators know that being the first to reveal their opening position puts them at a tactical disadvantage and on the defensive, which is better for you. Good negotiators avoid putting a number out until they have as much information as possible.

When I work with clients in negotiation situations, I always tell them this rule. But they almost always respond with the objection that it is difficult to get the other side to go first. In a situation like buying a car or something from Craigslist, the first offer is already out there so you have to take it from there.

Lucky for you, getting even the savviest negotiators to reveal their opening price is a skill that can be quickly learned. In any negotiation, one of your most powerful tools is a good question. And there are many you can use to draw the other side out. I've included a list of effective questions at the end of this section. I routinely use these questions, or some variation, to get the other side to open up.

Even a sticker price that is clearly written on a car-window invoice is not fixed and I would argue that it is not actually the dealership's starting position. I always ask how firm the sticker (dealer invoice) price is before beginning to haggle. And most times I get at least a 5-percent discount right off the bat. This is a much better place to start.

(Negotiating tip: When a car dealer shows you the "dealer invoice" to prove how good a deal you are getting, be wary. "Dealer invoices" are regularly generated by the car manufacturer to provide dealers with a negotiation tool. Although the number may actually be the amount the dealership is charged by the manufacturer, it is most likely not the amount the dealership will pay for the car. These official looking pieces of paper do not reflect the discounts and incentives the dealers receive on top of the listed price. You can pretty much ignore that number and keep negotiating.)

Before you provide an opening price or position, there are a couple of things you should know. The first is how much value your product or service provides to your customer. The value your customer puts in your product or service is one of the most important indicators of your negotiation leverage. For instance, if you have a highly differentiated product or service with few or limited number of competitors then that gives you substantial leverage, especially if you know that the customer has bought into its value proposition. If you know the advantages your product has over the competition, then you have more leverage.

The reason you want the other side to go first is because that gives you the option to reconsider your opening position. As part of your strategy, you take the time to compare your confidential initial price to the other side's opening position. This can help you decide whether you have enough negotiating room and whether your starting point is too high or too low.

There are times, however, that you run into a customer who has no idea what might be a reasonable price. You might then lead with the price as a way of educating him or her. But remember that we are dealing with a tough customer, one who likes playing these games.

Another point: I often encounter salespeople who believe that their job doesn't require negotiation skills. They tell me that they don't have any say with pricing, that most of their prices are negotiated at a national level by people higher up in the organization. That may be true. But keep in mind that though the price might be fixed, there are many other things that are not. Sample product, terms and conditions, and guaranteed usage quantities, for example, are all things that are negotiable; and if you are facing a hardball negotiator, expect them to be put into "play." Tough customers always want their "pound of flesh," which isn't always measured in dollars and cents. Many things other than price make up a deal.

A hardball negotiator who really needs a one-of-a-kind product and has little leverage to get a reduced price will still push for other concessions like payment terms, shipping costs, delivery schedule, and so on. Tough customers will let you have your price, but cherry-pick in other areas to improve their side of the bargain. So keep in mind that although prices may be fixed, that doesn't necessarily mean that you don't negotiate other parts of a deal.

But getting the customer to put the number out there first can create an ethical dilemma for some.

I have a client who practices this technique very successfully in the wealth management business. One of the tools for wealth transfer is the use of large life insurance policies that allow for intergenerational wealth transfer with substantially less tax penalties.

(Ever hear of something called Stranger Owned Life Insurance, or STOLI? As long as you agree to it, a person or corporation who does not know you can take a life insurance policy out on you for millions of dollars, paying your hefty premiums and collect when you kick the bucket. There are some interesting goings-on in the wealth management transfer business.)

Most of these policies come with a hefty premium, as you can imagine. When designing one of these insurance strategies, the financial advisor is usually given a range of premiums by the insurance underwriter. So the client can quote the high-net-worth individual anywhere along this range. Usually, my client has a number in mind, but is reluctant to communicate it before the investor lets him know his or her budget. And sometimes, the investor's budget is substantially higher than the number my client had in mind.

You can clearly see the advantage of this technique in this situation. The ethical question is "What would you do?" Would you raise the number you originally had in mind, ensuring more profit for yourself and your firm, or would you stick with your original number as a "fair" premium?

We can safely assume that in similar situations, most hardball negotiators don't feel the same amount of remorse as most win-win players would about raising their price. After all, there is a very popular negotiating book available that flouts the idea that "You don't get what you deserve, you get what you negotiate." In zero-sum negotiations, the idea of reaching a "fair" agreement is not something tough opponents often take into consideration.

I was involved in a negotiation with a client over the resale of semiconductor manufacturing equipment a couple of years ago. My client was trying to negotiate pricing with the company reselling the equipment and I was helping them reach a deal.

In a preliminary meeting, we asked the sellers how much they originally paid for the equipment. We were pretty sure that, in the depressed market of three years earlier, they must have had a substantial discount. We wanted to avoid basing our opening bid on the full list price at the time the sellers acquired the equipment.

They responded to our question with "We don't think the original price is relevant to our discussions. We prefer to focus on how much the equipment is worth today."

At first, my client capitulated: "Okay, we understand."

That's no way to play tough! I pulled them out of the room for a sidebar.

"Wait," I said. "You can't roll over that easy. You have to push them to reveal the amount they paid. The price they originally paid is relevant to how much we offer. But it does put them in a weaker negotiating position if they reveal it. Let's put some pressure on them and see what happens."

We reentered the negotiation and explained that the original price was very relevant and we needed to know it before going any further. We held our ground and eventually, and with much reluctance, they revealed that the price the company paid for the equipment three years ago was 20 percent below list price. Had I allowed my client to knuckle under so quickly, we would have given away that 20 percent right from the get-go.

There is an art to skilled negotiation. It isn't as simple as asking the other side the question and moving on. When dealing with tough negotiators, you have to be persistent.

Here are some questions I typically ask to get the other side to put their number on the table first:

"Is this a budgeted item? If so, can you share your budget with me?"

"Do you have a number in mind? If so, can you give me an idea of how much?"

"Can you give me a ballpark figure to begin with?"

"What do you think this is worth?"

"Do you have an idea of the approximate cost?"

"Is there a range you are looking to stay within?"

"Is there a number you are trying to stay under (or over)?"

"When you bought something similar in the past, how much did you pay?"

"IIow long have you had your current product? Can you tell me how much it cost originally?"

"Can you tell me where the competition is pricing their proposal?"

As for getting them to reveal their opening position first, expect tough customers to keep their cards close to the vest in almost all situations. So expect resistance. A worthy opponent will refuse to answer your questions or, even craftier, will answer a question with a question.

You ask, "Well, what do you think it is worth?" and they reply, "I don't know. What do *you* think it is worth?"

You ask, "Do you have a price in mind?" and the other side responds with "Well, do you have a budget you need to stay within?"

The best response to a negotiator's parroted question is always a more sophisticated version of "I asked you first!"

The following are some samples.

Their Question: "Well, just give me a ballpark price so I can have something to work with."

Your Response: "Sure, but can you give me an idea of the number you have in mind?"

Their Question: "What do *you* think it's worth?"

Your Response: "I don't know. Did you have an approximate cost target in mind?"

Their Question: "Do you give a volume discount?"

Your Response: "Well, how large a volume are we talking? And did you have an idea of the amount of discount you are looking for?"

Their Question: "Is there a number you are trying to stay under (or over)?"

Your Response: "I have a number, but I'd like to get your take first."

Be careful how you answer questions from the other side. Once you find yourself on the defensive, tough negotiators won't back off, like in this exchange:

The buyer asks, "Do you ever give 90-day payment terms?"

The salesperson replies, "No, we don't like to extend the payments out further than 30 days."

And the buyer, smelling blood in the water, replies, "Well you said you don't like to. But I asked if you ever do it?"

To this, the salesperson answers, "Well, it has to be a special case for us to do that."

The buyer pounces: "So you do it, but only in cases that you think warrant special consideration."

"Um . . . I guess."

You can see where this is going.

Stop and think before responding to questions in any negotiation, especially with negotiators playing hardball.

#2: Make them defend their number.

Getting your opponent to reveal their opening position can put them on the defensive, but challenging them to defend their number once they put it on the table can push them even further off their game plan. Once the other side reveals his or her number, you challenge them to defend it. This is seldom done and can catch tough opponents by surprise, especially if he or she hasn't thought through the answer.

Tough negotiators are seldom prepared for this tactic because they mostly pull their starting numbers out of their . . . er, head. And because their opening strategy is often predictable, you can usually assume that they will low-ball you and start with the opening position, which gives them the largest amount of negotiating margin.

A couple of years ago, I was looking to replace the engine of my Toyota 4-Runner. I loved the SUV, but with more than 200,000 miles it had lost most of its get up and go.

I priced a new replacement engine on the Toyota Parts and Service Website as one option. Toyota wanted $4,500 for a brand-new, factory-built engine. Now I enjoyed this car a lot, but their price was more than I was prepared to pay to continue this pleasure.

By luck, I found one on Craigslist from a local Seattle private party advertising the engine for $1,500. The ad listed a phone number and a name, Adolph. So I called the number. (Adolph seemed about the same age as me, 50, at the time. I could be wrong, but I don't know many parents who would choose Adolph as a name for their child in 1955. But I called Adolph with a bit of caution.)

I introduced myself and asked about the engine. He told me it was in excellent condition, having been driven only 10,000 miles. Adolph said he had a local mechanic who would vouch for the engine's condition.

He was clear that he didn't want to negotiate the price. "You saw on my ad that my price is firm, right?"

"Yes, I noticed that," I said, giving him little indication of whether it had any effect on me. "Do you mind if I ask you a question about the price?"

"You can, but I'm not budging." Adolph was already getting testy.

"I know, I know. I just want a little more information if that's okay with you?"

"Fine, but my price is firm."

"Do you mind sharing with me how you arrived at the price for the engine?"

"Whaddya mean?"

"Well, you seem pretty fixed on the $1,500 for the engine, so I was thinking that you most likely did your homework on its market value," I replied.

"I figured it's in good shape and I haven't seen any others for sale online, so I figured I could get $1,500 for it."

"So I guess the $1,500 price is something you came up with on your own."

"That's right. But it don't matter. The price is the price, take it or leave it."

"Well, it seems like a lot of money for something if you can't verify its true market value. I might have to take a pass."

Then Adolph shared much more information than he should have. He gave me a sob story trying to appeal to my more human nature:

"Well, to be honest with you [which automatically made me think that he wasn't], I am moving from Seattle to Texas with my family and we need the money to help with moving expenses."

In that short statement Adolph told me two things: First, and actually the lesser-important fact, was that he was most likely a motivated seller; I assumed most people would not want to drag an engine from the Northwest to the Southwest if they could avoid it.

His second, and much more important revelation, was that Adolph did not know what the engine was worth. By basing his defense on appealing to my more human nature he left himself wide open.

This offered me a distinct advantage—and another ethical dilemma.

Let's deal with the distinct advantage first.

Not having a logical explanation of how he arrived at the engine's price, Adolph put himself in a position that was difficult to defend. If he'd done his research and knew the price of the factory engine he'd have been able to say, "You know, Steve, a new engine of this quality will cost you at least $4,500, plus shipping and handling," which would have been a much better argument than the sob story about his expensive move to Texas. He would have been in a much better negotiation position and perhaps gotten more for the engine, or at least I would have had to fight harder to get him to reduce his price. But without a credible argument for the $1,500 price, I had the upper hand.

I offered him $700 and he took it immediately. Talk about capitulating. If he had been even a marginally better negotiator, he should have countered my lowball offer at least once. He would have ended up with more because my options were limited. There were not many engines on the market for this auto.

Now for the ethical dilemma.

One reason I enjoy writing and lecturing on negotiation is because the topic inevitably raises ethical questions that provide enlightenment into human morals and mores.

When I tell the "Adolph" story to other people, their responses typically fall into one of two categories. About half of the people smile and tell me that I paid too much for the engine even at $700. They argue that because Adolph was in the middle of a move, I had him over a barrel and could have offered him anything and he would have taken it. I'm not so sure about that.

The other half say that because the engine is truly worth more and Adolph is in a difficult situation, it would be unfair to take advantage of him. They say that I should be generous and pay him what he wants, the full $1,500, that it is a fair deal.

The Adolph situation presented me with an ethical quandary that could result in two very different negotiation outcomes. Do I take advantage of my leverage in the situation and offer Adolph a lowball price, a price even below the $700, or do I have sympathy for the guy and pay his full asking price of $1,500?

Did I take advantage of Adolph by offering $700? I don't believe so. Was it a win-win? I don't think Adolph would say that. Did his hardball approach work out for him? It actually worked against him. The key negotiation point is that regardless of how you view the situation, it is clear that had Adolph been better able to defend his position, I would have paid more for the engine.

The rest of the story went like this:

Once Adolph and I had closed the deal, I drove my SUV to his house to pick up the engine. After heaving it onto the truck, Adolph asked me if I'd like to have a beer and sit for a minute. I accepted and shared with him that I had lived in Texas during my first job after graduate school. I asked if he was looking forward to moving to a warmer, sunnier climate.

"Actually, we are looking forward to the move. My wife's folks live in Dallas and we are both sick and tired of the rain in Seattle."

Then he added a final thought, in a bragging, sort of show off tone, but without really thinking about it.

"And get this, GM wrote us a blank check of $25,000 for the move and it isn't even costing us half that much. So I'm taking my family on a cruise for two weeks with the rest."

Apparently, Adolph didn't remember using the sob story to try and get me to pay $1,500 for the engine. Now, if I had paid him his full asking price I would have been steamed. But something tells me that if I'd paid Adolph his original asking price, he also would have never told me about the check from General Motors.

The thorny question this story raises is whether you negotiate the best deal possible for your side regardless of the carnage you leave in your wake, or whether you negotiate the best deal for both parties. I think this is a fair question. Just because you know how to play hardball doesn't mean you should always use those skills. When I am at a flea market or craft fair, I usually pay full price because I know that these people have families to feed and bills to pay. But when it comes to people, especially people using hardball techniques, I feel little to no remorse for getting a deal that mostly favors my interests over theirs.

For the purposes of this particular negotiation book, we are assuming that tough negotiators want the best deal for their side at the expense of yours, whether fair or unfair. And, like I learned from Adolph (after the fact), it is hard to know going into a negotiation whether someone is playing win-win and is actually revealing his interests to you, or if someone is playing zero-sum and will bend the truth to get a profitable deal.

I am involved in many negotiations in which the other side seems cooperative and friendly only to find out that they were using the relationship as a tactic to get concessions I would not have otherwise given. Last year I went with a friend to a "no haggle" car dealership to familiarize myself with their approach. The salesperson was nice, the sales manager was nice, and even the finance guy seemed nice until the document signing. Before providing the final papers to sign, he pulled out an extended warranty attempting to pressure my friend into buying coverage he didn't want or need.

When I counseled my friend to turn it down, the finance manager insisted that he needed a signature on the warranty stating that my friend understood that he was declining the coverage. I told the finance manager that if he wanted the deal he would have to do it without my friend's signature. He quickly realized that this was deal breaker and backed down. (I also posted a Yelp review telling everyone to expect this tactic at that dealership. It's the 98 percent of crooked car dealers that give the other 2 percent a bad name.) I have no idea what dealers are thinking when they pull this kind of bush-league, amateur trick. I suppose because they work on most people.

So when it comes to honesty, I stick to tactics I feel are fair in all situations and work effectively whether in a win-win or zero-sum negotiation. Getting the other side to defend their price is a fair tactic against either approach.

Like I said in the introduction for this book, I try to make my approach as user-friendly and easy to remember as possible. Keeping in that vein, I have some questions I use to test the other side's number once I get them to put it on the table. As with Adolph, having a couple of simple, useful questions can change the outcome significantly:

"How did you come up with that number? How did you come up with your first offer?"

"Why did you start with such a low/high number?"

"How did you arrive at that?"

"I don't understand your reasoning. Can you help me by explaining how you came up with it?"

"That number seems like a lot to ask for; can you tell me what you based it on?"

I've heard some pretty illogical defenses through the years, like "Well, I just feel it is worth that much," or "I still owe money on it," or even "I knew you were going to start high so I started low."

Using questions to force the other side to step back and defend their position is a crucial first step in weakening their opening position and strengthening yours. Tough negotiators don't expect it because it is rarely done and, even more rarely, done well.

To soften them up even more, push them to reveal whether or not their number is flexible. A tough negotiator will almost always position their number as "firm." But sometimes you can get a sense of the negotiator's flexibility by asking:

"How firm are these prices/terms/conditions?"

"Do you have any room to move? In which areas: price, terms, or conditions?"

"Are these numbers firm or negotiable?"

If you can get them to answer any of those questions, remember:

"Or best offer (O.B.O.)" means they have a lot of room to maneuver.

"Negotiable" means they have some room to maneuver.

"Firm" doesn't mean they have no room to maneuver; it simply means you will have to work harder to get them to give ground.

The only time you should consider putting your number on the table first with a tough negotiator is if your number is fixed and you have no room to lower or raise the price. But that really isn't a negotiation because, by definition, negotiation is the back-and-forth. If your price really "is what it is," then there is no back-and-forth and thus no negotiation.

Here is a valid point that sales managers will appreciate. Many salespeople complain that they don't have the authority to negotiate. They complain that without the authority to make a final deal, they are put into a weak negotiating position by their management. Now, there are two very clear sides to this argument. First, I see many salespeople tell customers that they will need to run the figures by their managers as a tactic to give them some time to think about the deal on the table. This is not a particularly bad tactic.

The second point is that there are situations in which it is not in your interest to have the power to finalize a deal.

Let me use the hospital/health insurer example again if I may. Often in the final phase of a negotiation, the upper management of the health plan will get involved in the negotiation process because of the business critical decisions that need to be made and because they want to protect their contract negotiators from making decisions that might jeopardize both the deal and the negotiator's career. Although it can be argued that having all the authority to cut whatever deal you feel the need to cut gives you more negotiating freedom, it can also be more responsibility than a salesperson wants or can handle. Sometimes, you want management to make the decisions.

At the same time, keep this in mind. When you use the lack of negotiation authority as an excuse and not a tactic, such as telling a customer, "You know, mister customer, I agree that our prices are too high, but what can I do? My hands are tied," you are weakening your negotiation position, not improving it. The phrase "Our prices are fair and reasonable, and let me tell you why" communicates to the customer that you are the person in charge of the deal and that they will need to negotiate with you before getting any concession. This includes the concession of escalating the negotiation to your manager's level.

If you spend enough time in my profession, you run into many people who may think they are talented negotiators, but who really are not. A couple of years ago I was in competition with another negotiation expert to create a seminar for a medical device client.

In one of our last meetings before the vendor selection was decided, I had the VP of sales say to me in a clumsy attempt to get me to reduce my fees, "Steve, I have to let you know that your competition really wants this business and is aggressively discounting their fees to win the contract." I then asked if he would allow me to see their proposal, which he refused.

He then said, in an even clumsier attempt, "I should let you know that your competition said that they will do whatever it takes to get our business." He added, "Whatever it takes."

That stopped me for a second. But after thinking it through, I asked him quizzically, "Do you really think that this guy can make your salespeople better negotiators when he's already told you that they will do anything to get your business?"

He thought for a minute.

"Oh yeah. I don't think we would."

#3: Defend your price.

Defending your opening number is critical to reaching better agreements. Apply this to the Adolph story. Without a solid explanation for the reasons behind his price for the engine, he was immediately on the defensive.

If Adolph responded to my challenge by saying, "Well, I looked at the retail price of $4,500, then subtracted a bunch because of the 10,000 miles and the fact that I'd like to make a quick sale, and decided that $1,500 was a fair and reasonable price for an engine in this good of a condition," I would have been on the defensive immediately.

But he didn't, so I wasn't.

The key to successfully defending your position relies on your ability to do two things. First, have a rational explanation of how you arrived at your opening price. Second, provide a convincing argument that your product is worth the price. To successfully defend your price, you must be able to answer the following questions clearly and confidently: "How did you arrive at your price?" or "What did you base it upon?" and "Why should I pay more for your product? What makes it worth the amount you are asking?"

Solid responses to these questions make it much harder for tough negotiators to make headway against your position.

Let's deal with the first question.

I had a client in a national contract negotiation ask the other side, "How did you arrive at your pricing model in your opening RFP?" They explained that one of their assumptions was that our side would start much higher, so they lowballed us to offset those pressures. It is difficult to hold your ground when you are basing your defense on the other side's offense.

But a good answer should put the other side on the defensive.

As for the second question, "Why should I pay more for *your* product than your competition?" you must be able to convince the other side that your offering is more valuable than their alternatives.

A logical explanation of how you arrived at your opening price *and* a strong value proposition are very powerful first steps in resisting pressure to reduce your price.

For argument's sake, though, let's consider this from the customer's perspective. The only way for the customer to close the gap between the higher price you want to charge them and the low price they want to pay is to either convince you that your product isn't worth the difference or get you to make concessions until you reach the amount they are willing to pay.

The other side's job is to convince you, the seller, that your product is a commodity that brings little to no added value from your competition. The reasoning is that if they can convince you that your product is no different than your competition, you have less leverage. As I said, the most damaging mistake you can make is to buy into the customer's belief that your product or service is a commodity. A salesperson who doesn't believe that his or her product, service, or company brings more value than the competition will be a poorer negotiator.

I see quite a lot of salespeople let buyers commoditize their product or service without putting up a fight. Sometimes, this can be deceptively effective and deceptively challenging to pull off.

One of my clients is a manufacturer of heavy construction machines. Their purchasing department recently contacted me to discuss my contract renewal for the upcoming year. The client had an issue with the wording of the cancellation clause in my standard contract.

All my contracts include a 30-day cancellation clause to protect me from last-minute shifts in client priorities and interruptions in my cash flow. This client contacted me with the intention of removing the clause wording from my current contract.

After introducing himself, the contracts administrator said, "Mr. Reilly, we'd like you to consider removing the cancellation clause in your contract."

I asked him why it was an issue at that time, as all my previous contracts contained the clause.

The contract negotiator replied, "Well, we are expecting a tough year, so we need to reduce our financial exposure wherever possible."

I agreed that risk management is important, but stated that I wanted to explain my side of the dilemma.

"Well, let's suppose one of your customers agrees to buy a bulldozer and at the last minute cancels the order. Do you mind my asking what you would do in that situation?"

"Well, we certainly don't charge the customer for the machine, if that's what you mean," he replied.

"Right, but what do you do with the bulldozer?"

"What do you mean, 'What do we do with the bulldozer?'"

"Well, do you sell it to someone else?" I asked.

"Well, yeah, if we get another customer for it. We put it back in storage until someone else comes in looking for this type of machine."

"Precisely. But my services are different. When you cancel an order with me at the last minute, I don't have a 'bulldozer' to sell to someone else, if you know what I mean. When you cancel my consulting work at the last minute, rarely can I find another client to pay me for that time."

Frustrated, the accounting person said, "Well, all I know is that you are the only consultant we work with who has a cancellation clause in the contract and we need consistency."

What would your next move be? Would you accept the argument and eliminate the clause? Would you refuse and risk losing a valuable customer?

My response is not one typically heard by "buyers" in a customer negotiation:

"Well, with all due respect, the services I offer are different from other consultants and let me tell you why."

In the end, I was able to keep the clause in my contract for another year at a minimum.

But by using this tactic, I risked the client saying, "Well, we will just use other consultants then." To mitigate this risk, I had to make my argument strong enough to convince the purchasing person that my value was substantial enough to allow the clause as an "exception."

Understand that a "buyer" will attempt to make your offering as generic as possible, often without thinking. It gives them an edge. Your job is to make the argument that your product or service is different and better.

Another useful scenario would be the used car example I used earlier. If you remember, the car was listed for $17,000 and the Kelley Blue Book price is $15,000. Let's also say that you bought this car new and are the only person to ever drive it; in car-speak you have what is called an "A" title. And let's say you are making your "pitch" to the interested party about the quality of your car and add to the list of items: "By the way, this car has an 'A' title. So, you know, I was the only owner and sole driver."

The other party then replies, "I don't care how many people owned this car. I still don't want to pay $17,000!"

A less-skilled negotiator's response might be "Well, would you be willing to pay me $16,500 then?" This would be your second mistake of negotiation—conceding $500 and getting nothing for it.

A tougher response is "But you should care about having an 'A' title and let me tell you why. It is in your best interest to get a car from someone who has knowledge of how the car was treated because . . ."

In the same vein, when a customer or purchasing agent asks you, "Is this the best price you can give me?" or "Can you do any better on the price?" the wrong response is "Let me talk to my manager and get back to you." All that communicates is that you are not the person to negotiate with. The better response to a customer's request for a lower price is not a counteroffer, but rather the phrase "This is a good price and let me tell you why."

Again, if we measure a negotiation's success by how close your final deal is to your opening price, a good beginning is a solid argument intended to convince the other side that your product or service is not a commodity. Do not give up your opening price without a good fight.

Tough negotiators will make you and your products "the worst" in order to increase their leverage. They'll complain about your product, your service, and your price, using whatever it takes to get an edge. They will debunk even the most valid value arguments.

Try not to take this personally. Consider it their job. It's their job to argue that your product is a commodity, of equal or lesser quality than your competitors, and is not valuable at all. Your job is to argue that your product is differentiated, is high quality, and is of high value. They position problems, you position benefits; they position similarities, and you position uniqueness. You look them in the eye and defend your product, service, and price.

Your profitability depends on the quality and confidence of your argument. Sell value before making any concessions. But defending your position takes moxie and chutzpah, and can entail risks.

Now, returning to an issue I mentioned earlier. Previously I said that many salespeople complain that management limits their ability to negotiate, that sales managers hold the negotiating power and make all the pricing decisions. But I also see the same salespeople in a negotiation tell the customer, "This is the best price my manager will allow me to give you. Management makes the pricing decisions."

This statement seriously erodes your negotiating power.

Even if it's true that management holds the ultimate negotiating power, when you negotiate you want the person sitting across the table to think you are the heavy, the muscle. You create a more power-ful negotiation position for yourself by making the case for the value of your product, not by using man-agement's approval to resist customer demands.

By using the phrase "This is a fair and reasonable price and let me tell you why," you communicate that you are the one making the decisions, that they will have to get past you and your argument before they get anything in return—including the opportunity to talk to your manager.

This is easier in some situations than others. It would be nice to always have a truly unique, highly differentiated product so you have the upper hand in a negotiation. But more often, salespeople find themselves up against hardball negotiators who make even the most unique product seem like a commodity.

This doesn't mean you can't reach a profitable agreement if your product truly is a commodity; you just need to be very good at trading concessions.

You Are a Better Negotiator Already

Here is a situation I found myself in a number of years ago. Based on what you've read so far, try to figure out how you would approach the same situation.

On a recent Friday afternoon, I returned home from working with one of my clients on the east coast. I had a workshop with a local Seattle company scheduled for Monday morning and needed copies of the materials that accompany the class. In my line of work, you make a lot of copies: copies of training workbooks, copies of project planners, copies of client materials. Not far from my house is a FedEx Kinko's copy center. I use it on a regular basis because it's close and convenient.

On my way back from the airport, I stopped at Kinko's with the workbook originals and requested 50 copies by Sunday afternoon. The counter person informed me that because of the heavy workload and lack of staff, they could not produce the copies in time to meet my deadline. A bit disconcerted, as this had never happened before, I asked about alternatives.

The clerk told me the Kinko's University store could meet my printing deadline because they had the large staff required by University of Washington students who typically do things at the last minute. Reluctant to drive all the way to the University district (10 miles, 20 minutes), I asked that the clerk call and make sure. He made the call for me and determined that they could have the copies ready by

Sunday morning if I was able to deliver the master copy to them by that afternoon.

I drove the distance and dropped off the copies with the assurance that the production job would be ready by Sunday morning. Then I drove home and enjoyed my weekend.

The "Negotiation"

On Sunday morning, I returned to the University Kinko's and the clerk handed me the completed materials and a bill for $500.

As is my usual routine, I asked if he might be able to give me a volume discount. "I'm not sure, but this seems like a larger order and bill than is typical for Kinko's. Can you do a little something for me on the price?"

Confused, the clerk asked me what I meant.

"Well, I do a lot of business at Kinko's and I was wondering if you might give me a discount for such a big order?"

The clerk paused, and then asked me to wait while she got the manager. She returned in a minute with Greg, the store manager. He asked how he could help.

I explained my situation in a very friendly way and, after telling him that I did quite a lot of business with FedEx Kinko's throughout the year, reiterated my request for some sort of discount.

Greg smiled and replied, "Well, I think we can do something since you are such a good customer. How would a 20-percent discount sound?"

"Great," I replied and pulled out my credit card.

Greg knocked $100 off the invoice, and I took my box of materials and happily returned home for Sunday breakfast, thinking to myself, "That Greg is a nice guy."

Then I thought about it, asking myself the question, "Why did Greg give me a $100 discount?"

Perhaps he is just a nice guy. More likely, he probably thought that I would repay his good deed with loyalty and bring more copying work to his store. But as a small business owner who often has to produce workbooks on short notice, while keeping a sharp eye on the bottom line, my loyalty is often based on how much it costs to run my business. Thus, giving a steep discount in exchange for goodwill is not usually a good negotiation strategy—at least not with me.

Also, think about who had the leverage in this situation. Greg had the materials that I needed for my Monday workshop. I was on the other side of the counter, without my materials. Who has the upper hand?

To be fair, Greg is a Kinko's store manager and not a professional negotiator. Unlike professional or habitual negotiators, most people probably don't ask for a discount at a copy store, so Greg likely doesn't get much negotiating experience.

But an important factor that can influence amateur and professional negotiators alike is whether they are negotiating with their own money. In this situation, Greg wasn't and I was. He was using Kinko's money and had little to nothing to lose. His role as a store manager is likely based on customer satisfaction, not profit margin. If Greg were being compensated based on the store's profitability, I doubt he would have been so generous.

So let's see if you can apply some of the things covered so far in the book.

Put yourself in the same position as Greg, the store manager. I come into your store to pick up my print job and ask if you can provide me a discount on such a large job. What would be a better response than "Sure, how about 20 percent off the cost of the job?"

There is more than one right way to conduct a negotiation, but you would have done better than Greg if your response to my request for a discount was something like "How much of a discount did you have in mind?" I might ask for a 20-percent discount and a counter of 10 percent would net you and your store $50 more in profit.

Another option would be to ask me about the volume of my Kinko's business and then negotiate a volume discount based upon future purchases. You could then promise a discount on the next purchase and give me your business card with the discount written on it.

In fact, what Greg did was avoid the negotiation: He capitulated to my request without any negotiation.

Here's the rest of the story:

Two weeks later, as is the nature of my business, I found myself in a similar situation. I needed a quick turnaround on printing workshop materials late in the week. Anticipating the problem with the previous job, I made a point of getting the materials to my local Kinko's (not the University Kinko's) on Thursday (not Friday). This time, the clerk told me the printing would be ready Sunday morning. I thanked him and returned home.

Sunday morning, I returned to pick up my materials and when presented with the bill, I told the clerk, "When I use the University Kinko's, Greg, the manager, gives me a 20-percent discount on big orders." Without hesitation he calculated 20 percent off the invoice, revised my bill, and took my check. A successful transaction completed—at least, successful on my end.

Now, some people reading this might see my tactic as unethical and unfair, but that is too thorny an issue to discuss at this point. I tell this story not to wander into an ethical quagmire, but to remind the reader of the two most common mistakes made over and over again by negotiators in every company, in every industry, by every one of my clients, and of course by Greg.

Poor negotiators give ground too easily and get nothing in return.

Greg gave me $100 directly from his bottom line and received nothing in return: no loyalty, no promise of business, nothing but my "thanks." I give him a lot of credit for being a nice guy, but he could still be a nice guy and get more for his $100.

(By the way, for those of you thinking of trying this at your local Kinko's, they've since implemented a volume discount policy that assigns and tracks a Kinko's account number and automatically calculates a discount based on annual purchase volume. I now make my copies at OfficeMax, which has its own version of Greg.)

THREE

Counteroffers

Trading, Not Making, Concessions

The customer was definitely in the position of wanting my client's technology: a new and sophisticated microchip testing process that included software, hardware, quite a bit of post-sale service, and support packages. The technology would improve quality and reduce down-time and manufacturing costs. But in spite of a clear and measurable competitive advantage and value to the customer, my client's salesperson caved early.

"So your product is more expensive than the technology we currently use. Can you help me out with the price? I might be able to get my people to commit to the purchase if you can discount it by 20 percent. Can you do that for me?" asked the customer.

"I'm not allowed to discount this product, but how about if we split the cost of the installation? Would that help?" replied the salesperson.

"Maybe," the customer responded. "But I'll have to talk my team and get back to you."

I butted in. "If you don't mind, can I ask a question regarding your decision-making process?"

"Uh, sure," said the customer. She looked a bit confused because I was only a consultant working with the manufacturer's salesperson in the field; I was not a representative of his company.

"You said earlier that this technology provides a significant advantage over your current semiconductor test methodology. Is that right?" I asked.

"Yes, we've run the benchmark testing and it is clear that it gives us some efficiencies over how we've done things in the past," she said hesitantly, not knowing where I might be going with this line of questioning.

"So you feel that the new process brings both quantitative and qualitative value to you and your company. Am I correct?"

"Yes, our numbers show a reduction in errors and longer uptime for the fabrication process."

"And do the other decision-makers realize the improvement in MTBF [Mean Time Between Failures] and that impact of savings and efficiencies gained by my client's products?" I asked.

The customer's eyes narrowed as I sensed apprehension building in her. She then asked, "So I expect that you want me to pay for the installation instead of splitting the costs with your client?"

"No, I'm not saying that. I am asking that because his company is going to absorb half of the installation costs, can you agree to having the evaluation done by the end of the month?"

"That seems reasonable."

"Then we have a deal?" I asked.

"Yes, I believe we have a deal."

Counteroffers Strategy

The all-too-common belief about negotiation is that you shouldn't give any ground at all—that holding your ground at all costs makes you a talented negotiator. I agree with this up to a point. But a well-thought-out concession strategy can gain you more than you might get from simply refusing to negotiate.

However, even though having a strong advantage over your competitors does give you a negotiating advantage, the fact remains that there are some products and services that are pretty generic. Although wire cable by the ton can be pretty difficult to differentiate, some products have significant advantages and a strong stand-alone value proposition.

The good news is that even if your company's product or service doesn't have much of a competitive advantage, that doesn't mean you are in a weak negotiating position. All it means is that you have to get very good at trading concessions to ensure a better deal than you would if you only made concessions.

Defending your position with a clear, logical, and firm explanation of how you arrived at your opening price is key. That, combined with a convincing argument that the value your product or service offers is worth the difference in price, establishes a good strong starting point in any negotiation.

Often, though, that doesn't mean the customer pays list price, not if they are good at negotiating. Making a strong value argument only means that you will get more than you would if you hadn't made the value argument. Sometimes you have to keep your expectations reasonable.

Salespeople who do these things well force buyers to make a better argument. You, as the negotiator, take the offensive and force the other side to defend their position. Defending your opening number is the first and best way to ensure a more profitable outcome than your bottom line.

At some point, however, something has to give.

Once prices are on the table, in order for the negotiation to move forward, someone has to counter; everything prior to the first counteroffer is just defending and positioning. Unless someone offers something in trade, the negotiation isn't going anywhere because it never really started.

This is the core of negotiation: the back-and-forth, offer and counteroffer, give and take. Many sales representatives and many people, generally, struggle with this step for a couple of reasons.

Some are uncomfortable with the ambiguity of the process; they would rather have a quick deal for better or worse than "haggle." This haggling takes time, patience, and thought; they'd rather have a deal, even a bad deal, than play the game. (If you get a chance to see the haggling scene in Monty Python's *Life of Brian*, I highly recommend you do. Hilarious!)

Oh, and just so you know, the other side is hoping you feel that way. Typically, the quicker you reach agreement, the better the deal for one side or the other.

For others, the back-and-forth is scary because it can be adversarial and they fear being taken advantage of. They feel that offering and counteroffering is too much like an argument or fight. Once again, a tough negotiator enjoys the battle, so it is better if you get used to it. A thick skin helps.

Still others struggle because it seems like the "seedy" part of negotiation, too "car dealer-ish." It seems so because you are playing their game, the car dealer's game. But you have to respect a car dealer's negotiating skills.

For one or all of these reasons, many people avoid the back-and-forth. But this is in essence avoiding negotiation itself. Back-and-forth is negotiating and tough negotiators are very good at it. Thus, if you want to beat tough negotiators at their own game, the process doesn't stop after defending your opening position. You've got to keep working the deal.

As in the initial negotiation stage, the differences between win-win and zero-sum negotiation are apparent in the approaches to making concessions. In a win-win approach, both parties openly share their interests with each other in a noble attempt to collaboratively "problem solve."

Once interests are on the table, the negotiating parties create mutually agreeable solutions to satisfy each side's interests. The approach is cooperative.

William Ury uses a story of two people arguing in a library. The librarian comes over and asks if she can help. They tell her that the issue has to do with the window next to their table. One man wants the window open whereas the other wants it closed. The librarian takes the time to ask them both why they want what they want. The man who wants the window open says that he needs some fresh air whereas the other says he wants it closed because it is blowing his papers off the desk. As Ury tells it, the librarian thinks about it then opens a window on the other side of the room, which supposedly satisfies both parties. Ury illustrates with this story the idea that a compromise of a half-open window would not have satisfied either party and that knowing the motivation behind the demands enables the parties to reach a more mutually acceptable and creative agreement.

Now this is a nice little story that teaches a key point regarding the win-win approach. But if you apply the same scenario to a typical hardball situation, the one side doesn't care what or why the other person wants what he wants.

He just wants the damn window closed!

Win-win may be appealing, but it's not a very effective approach if the other side is trying to get as much from you as possible. Against a zero-sum negotiator, it is essential that you protect your interests from being leveraged against you.

Putting all of your interests on the table invites the other side to take advantage.

I have two retail clients in Seattle to whom I consult on a regular basis. Both focus on strong service, great products, and customer loyalty. My work with them is with their sourcing group, their buyers. I teach their buyers how to negotiate agreements that are fair for both sides.

At one point in my work with the purchasing groups, I realized both were using the same offshore supplier for basic materials. That didn't seem strange, as some of even the most basic materials in the clothing production process are only available from single sources. I had a chance to see the price both companies were paying for the exact same fabric at the exact same volumes. One client was paying a 30-percent premium over the other manufacturer's price. As I dug into this, it became apparent that the client with the best price approached the supplier from a cautious and fairly strong negotiation position. Their purchasing people were fair, but certainly focused on the benefit of the business relationship to their company's specific costs and delivery needs.

The other client who was paying the premium valued its "relationship" with its suppliers; the company saw its suppliers as partners in the business. This would have been all well and good had the supplier been playing the same game, which they weren't. Thus, the price was significantly higher.

Also, with the client paying the 30-percent premium, I learned that at times the supplier would request to ship the product earlier than was agreed upon so they could get it off their shelves. Even though it was inconvenient and changed the supply chain metrics, my client always agreed to the request in a gesture of goodwill.

When I asked the lower-paying client if they had the same experience, they said that they allow the supplier to ship product earlier all the time. But to do that the supplier has to provide an additional 2-percent discount as an early stocking fee.

This is a clear example of how playing win-win and sharing interests with a customer who is not playing the same game can hurt you. The supplier is clearly using the buyer's interests against them. This is the challenge with the overuse and overeagerness to achieve a win-win outcome when the other side doesn't necessarily reciprocate on its demands. The retailer with the better pricing was still willing to accommodate the early shipment, but asking for something in return like an early stocking fee was a "fair" trade.

Incredibly, even after I pointed out the price differences, my client continues to pay the higher premium because they think the advantages outweigh the disadvantages. They still feel that paying a premium and making allowances in the name of collaboration is worth the higher price. On the other hand, my client with the better price hasn't seen any erosion of loyalty or service based on taking a stronger negotiation position. They continue to enjoy lower sourcing costs and very good service. Once again, go figure.

I think this raises the question "Shouldn't I make concessions in return for 'goodwill?'" This is the idea behind win-win negotiating: that people are basically good and when given a chance will reciprocate in kind. Though this may be a noble philosophy, it is not a negotiation strategy. All too often I see salespeople make concessions with a vague notion that it will benefit them in the long run—that having "goodwill" might, just might, make the other side play nice. Goodwill is nice to have, but when up against a zero-sum negotiator, don't count on it.

Hardball negotiators often use promises of future business as leverage without any intention of delivering.

Beware of phrases like "Hey, c'mon, buddy. I promise you we will give you the first shot at future business as long as you cut me a deal here." Empty promises of future business are often forgotten or ignored; "things change" is the most common excuse.

When dealing with tough negotiators, only a clear agreement on reciprocal "goodwill" is acceptable: shipping charges for payment terms; post-sale service for additional volume. I would even discourage concessions for "goodwill" in win-win situations.

Remember Adolph? Although he really wasn't in a tough financial position, he played it that way in a bid to use my "goodwill" for some extra money. If I had given him his price based on his "sob story," I would have ended up with the shorter end of the stick. Sometimes a person isn't a "tough" negotiator so much as a "sneaky" negotiator.

What many salespeople fail to realize is that, in many negotiations, things other than price are often in play. When tough negotiators face a situation in which the product is so unique that they have little leverage to get a better price, they will look to get something—anything—in return. Maybe they'll look for favorable payment terms, free delivery, or a special return policy—something. This is a crucial misunderstanding to clear up before moving on to the rules of trading concessions. My medical device client with the strong value proposition has some customers that pay list price for their product. That doesn't mean they pay full price.

They ask for my client to split startup costs or ship some product "gratis" as an act of "goodwill." And I tell them that it isn't always appropriate to deny their customer requests. But always "trade" these requests for something that you feel is fair and reasonable.

Good salespeople are always negotiating and it is important to see negotiation as a key competency in your job.

I was in my investment counselor's office a number of months back talking about my assets and we discussed an investment I had with another brokerage house that was providing less than stellar returns. I asked him about moving it into one of his firm's funds with higher potential. He thought it was a good idea, so we completed the funds transfer for a substantial amount of money.

After completing the paperwork, I casually told him, "So, when my father was young, if he moved that much money into an investment, they would have given him something as a thank you."

My broker laughed and said, "Sure, like a toaster or something."

"Right," I replied, only half-joking, "like a toaster."

"Well, Steve, we haven't given out toasters in a long time," the broker said with good-natured sarcasm.

"I know. But you must have something to give clients in return for their business. I mean, you and your firm get up-front fees and commissions. All I get is a return after a year and that's only when and if the fund does well. But how about something now?"

"You're not serious, are you?" He looked incredulous.

"Well, even if it is some sort of promotional item or something, you know . . . for the effort," I said, doing my best Bill Murray.

He mumbled something and opened his desk drawer, which was literally crammed full of items like golf balls, pens, leather binders, Post-it note pads with embossed corporate logos, and all kinds of paraphernalia.

"You mean stuff like this?" he asked.

"Exactly!" I said.

He proceeded to hand me five exquisite pen and pencil sets, two leather binders—and the stuff kept coming.

I asked him, "Don't the investment houses make these things for you to give to your clients?"

"Yeah, but no one ever asks for them. It seems inappropriate to offer something like this in return for a financial investment."

"Well, I think if someone gives your firm this much money, they should at least get a pen, don't you think?"

We had a good laugh and my daughters got some nice pens for school.

Now this may seem petty, but the moral of this story is that if you're in the position to offer the customer anything—terms, conditions, after-sales service and/or support, or even a pen and pencil set—then you *do* negotiate! So begin to think of yourself as a negotiator. Think of negotiating as a critical part of your skill-set.

However, a word of warning: When negotiating with seemingly small "freebies," keep in mind the measure of a negotiator's success: how close the final deal is to your opening price. Think of price as fully burdened costs. If you get a good price, but give away service, support, and so on, the total profit of the deal will be less than you think.

Now that we've established that negotiating applies to you, we can move on to the rules for trading concessions.

So your strategy in this phase of the negotiation is to ensure you receive something of value whenever you make a concession. This brings up the questions "How much should I concede?" and "How much should I ask for in return?"

In order to get something of reciprocal value in return, it is important to identify the value of your concessions. This may seem simple, but it often isn't.

Let's deal with the first question, which is essentially about the amount of ground you give on your first counter. It's a good question and not one easily answered with an absolute, but the idea of "it depends" is not helpful, either. You have to be careful not to set a bad precedent.

If you give too much on your first counter, there is the possibility that the customer will perceive you as having attempted to gouge them with your first offer. Too much distance between your first offer and your first counter can not only damage trust, but also encourages the other side to be less than accommodating in its counteroffers as well. That is another reason that your first offer be defensible.

So your first counter should give a measurable piece of ground with a measurable piece reciprocated from the other side. *Reasonable* is the word I would use to describe an amount to concede. And a reasonable amount of give is something you have to decide.

But then you have to "sell" that to the other side as a "fair and reasonable" amount of ground.

I would say that a concession of less than 1 percent in value seems unreasonable, but a more-than-20-percent concession sends the message that you had more room to maneuver than reasonable and so may be gouging or taking advantage of a weaker opponent.

When up against a tough customer, however, a more-conservative concession with specific and measurable reciprocal concessions is probably the best choice.

I have two Seattle clients with very different approaches to negotiating. The one client makes software for the gaming market, whereas the other is a sporting goods retailer. From my experiences with both clients with time, I've come to realize that the buyers at the gaming company are tough negotiators, whereas the retailer likes to play win-win whenever it can. So when I get a request for a proposal from them, I give quite a bit of thought as to how I approach them from a pricing perspective.

Whenever I give the technology company a quote, if the company thinks I am the best vendor, I can be assured they will come back to me and try to negotiate a better deal. The retailer is very different.

With them, if my price is out of their parameters for what they consider "reasonable," instead of coming back to negotiate, they typically give the business to another vendor. You can imagine how this impacts my negotiating approach. I always give myself more room to maneuver with the tough gaming software company than I do with my retail client. And I always leave the door open for my retail client to negotiate by adding the caveat to my proposal "And if my pricing is outside of the normal parameters you might be considering in this RFP, I am happy to discuss other pricing and compensation options that you may not have considered."

Knowing the difference between the two companies is important to my negotiation strategy because it impacts which game I play. And I could only know this through experience in dealing with both companies over time. The good news is that most salespeople deal with regular, repeat customers giving them the opportunity to figure out how much maneuvering room they might need from one case to another.

So the next question to address is "How much should I ask for in return for my concession?" This brings up the subject of counteroffers.

The book *Getting to Yes* fails to address the idea of a counteroffer; in fact, the word is not even mentioned in the original publication. Neither do most of the other most popular negotiating books on the market today.

When leading the *Getting to Yes* associated workshop, I was asked repeatedly about the value of concessions and how to ensure profitability in deals that included back-and-forth. Once again, our canned answers failed to provide any true guidance to the workshop participants. I heard simplistic statements like "Win-win negotiation is about the back-and-forth sharing of interests and possible solutions, not offers and counteroffers."

Give me a break.

So one of the questions I sought to answer once I decided to look beyond the *Getting to Yes* philosophy

The Countering Process

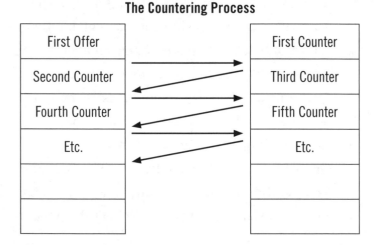

First Offer		First Counter
Second Counter		Third Counter
Fourth Counter		Fifth Counter
Etc.		Etc.

was "What is a concession worth?" I wanted to be able to answer this question from my clients with confidence and authority.

If you are going to concede the cost of more-generous payment terms, how much should you ask for in return? If you are going to cover the delivery costs, how much is that worth to the customer and how much is it worth to you? If your company provides post-sales training and support, how much is that worth?

These are big questions with a large impact on the profitability of a deal.

Some value is quantifiable. An extended warranty or better payment terms correlates directly to savings or revenue. Accounting departments can often calculate the true costs of different financing options or extended payments. When this is the case, I would recommend that your strategy should at least help cover your costs.

With many concessions, though, it can be difficult to validate true costs in terms of the overall negotiation because they are relative. The value of these hard-to-quantify items is often determined through the back-and-forth of the negotiation.

The best example for clarifying my point is to use a situation Caterpillar (CAT) runs into all the time. I refer to it as the "extra bucket dilemma."

Among myriad other products, CAT manufac-
tures and sells very high-quality backhoes used by
many companies in the construction industry. For
those of you unfamiliar with that business, a backhoe is a machine with a bucket on it used to scoop
large amounts of dirt and debris into the back of a
dump truck or out of the way. The "hoe" part of the
backhoe is in the back, thus the name.

Customers often ask the CAT dealership to "throw
in" an extra detachable bucket in case the teeth on
the original bucket break during the day-to-day wear
and tear of moving earth. It is a common practice to
ask for an extra bucket in that business, because if
a bucket breaks, a general contractor might have as
many as five or six people standing around (and being
paid) while waiting for the purchase and delivery of a
replacement bucket.

So consider these facts. The full retail price of a
bucket is about $1,500. However, the manufacturer's
cost is roughly $500, and the average price of a used
bucket, which are available from many sources, is
about $800. And the customer wants the extra bucket
for "free," of course. So the answer to the question
"How much is an extra backhoe bucket worth?" is
relative.

Let me explain the "relative" part.

The CAT salespeople, referred to as "Big Iron" reps, want to recover the cost of the bucket at least, right? But the value of the cost of a bucket is different depending on which replacement number you use: new retail, new wholesale, or used. So even though asking for something of at least equivalent "value" might seem straightforward, it is not always so. And here is the kicker.

Add to this equation the fact that the backhoe sells for $150,000, so the bucket is a small part of the larger deal. The CAT Big Iron rep has to take into consideration that refusing to throw in a "free bucket" just might cost the company a $150,000 sale. The "value" of a concession is not determined until you and the other side agree on what it is worth through the process of negotiation.

Now do you see how difficult it is to answer the question "How much should I get in return for a concession?"

So here is the answer I came up with to the question "How much should you get in return for the extra bucket?" *"As much as you can!"*

When a tough customer is forced to give something up, he or she will make you pay. The same should go for you. Get as much as you can for the smallest concession when up against a tough buyer.

If the concession has a quantifiable cost that needs to be recovered, that is one thing. However, when something is relative not just to the actual cost of the concession but to the overall success of the negotiation, then your strategy is to position and lobby for the amount you can defend! Get it?

This brings us to the first tactic in counter offering.

Concession Tactics

#1: Hard sell each concession.

Here is a situation I observed a number of years ago that illustrates the problem with being "too win-win."

My client was in a poor position relative to the competition while trying to complete the deal in front of us. The industry was price-sensitive with a high inelasticity of demand. (Remember that from your college economics? A high inelasticity of demand means that the customer is more likely to buy from someone else if the price increases.) The salesperson didn't have much leeway on pricing, but had quite a lot of flexibility in providing other value-added services. At this point in the negotiation, he was throwing everything but the kitchen sink into the deal. His approach seemed pretty desperate to me.

The salesperson made a desperate plea: "So how about if I give you the warranty and installation services for free. Would that get me the business?"

"Maybe," said the customer representative. "But can you sweeten the deal? I'd really like it if you would throw the shipping in as well. It's not that big an expense, so you can probably include that, too, right?"

"Okay. Let me see if I have this right. We will give you a 20-percent discount off list price, with the warranty, installation, and shipping for free. Can we close the deal now then?"

"Let me run this up the flag pole and see what my managers say. I'll get back to you."

"Uh, okay. I'll wait for your call. Thanks."

The first mistake the salesperson made was that he neglected to "sell" his concessions. Telling the customer that his company would provide them "free of charge" is a mistake, especially when dealing with a tough negotiator. And it is more than just a question of semantics.

It is important that when you make a concession, you make it "feel" like a concession to the other side.

In this situation, the salesperson built no value into his concessions. For some reason some sales-people make concessions seem of so little consequence to their company that the customer gets the idea that it isn't that big a deal and doesn't really cost the seller much. The result is that the buyer doesn't really feel as though he or she received that much value in the seller's concession. Making a big deal about concessions is a very important part of holding the line against tough bargainers.

Never, ever use the phrase *for free*, especially when dealing with tough negotiators. Never, ever tell a tough negotiator that something is "free," even things that technically are "free." This goes for every salesperson in every industry in every negotiation situation, period. Everything you give up has a cost, nothing is ever "no problem," and every concession should be traded for something against a tough negotiator. A good negotiator makes his or her opponent work for everything they give up.

Your company may provide post-sale service and support without charging the customer. But that doesn't mean it is "free." The key thing to remember is that your company is absorbing the costs for these services whether the customer pays for them or not.

Changing the phrase "We provide that to our customers free of charge" to "Our company absorbs the costs of this as added value to our customers" communicates to the customer that you are a business person with business interests.

The better way is to position your concessions by saying "Our company covers the costs of these valuable services" or "Our company absorbs the costs of these valuable services as part of the value we give to you" or "We pay for these services so you don't have to."

Holding your ground means intentionally positioning the value you bring as a defense against discounting. Companies spend money to create support and services as ways to increase the value of their products to the customer. And so, salespeople should recoup or at least use these "value-adds" as a way to defend your price.

I once heard a sales manager say jokingly that value-adds are things salespeople value, but only add cost to the sale. The things your company offers as additional ancillaries to a sale should never be positioned as "free."

This may seem petty. But in order to understand why this is not just a matter of word choice or semantics, let's replay this scenario with a different approach.

The salesperson says, "So you are asking my company to absorb the costs of the installation *and* the warranty. Did I get that right?"

The customer reply might be something like "That's right. You do want our business, don't you?"

"We want anyone's business as long as it makes sense to our company."

"So, can you do that for me?"

"We are already decreasing our profit margin by 20 percent, and on top of that you are asking us to cover the costs of installation and the warranty as well. That's a pretty unrealistic request, don't you think?"

"Well, how about just the warranty then?" asks the customer.

"I might be able to get my company to go for that, but only if we can get this deal done before the end of the month. Can you do that for me?"

By changing the added-value items of warranty and installation costs from "for free" to "absorbed costs," the salesperson increases the value of his offering, which results in the customer reducing his requests for "freebies." It is a simple and very effective technique.

Every concession should be hard-fought and hard-won. Just changing your response to a tough negotiator's demand from "I'll see what I can do" to "That's a lot to ask, especially when we are already absorbing the costs of a number of different items" lets the other side know that you will not give ground without a fight. The harder the other side has to fight, the better the deal for you.

So sell every concession as much as you can. The harder you sell it, the tougher it is for the other side to push you: Play it for all it's worth. Use a phrase such as "You can't be serious. I mean, we are barely making money on this deal. However, I am willing to see what I can do if you can throw me a bone or something to offset your request."

Consider this situation. I ask a salesperson for a lower price and he or she tells me, "I'll talk to my manager and see what I can do." The salesperson comes back later and tells me, "I tried, but my manager wouldn't go for it." I, of course, will be disappointed (which I would play for some other concession. See how this goes?). However, if when I ask for a lower price and the salesperson instead responds with "You're killing me here! We don't usually discount this product. But because of your willingness to be reasonable, I will go back to my management and go to bat for you. I will take this as high up in the chain of command as I can and push until they at least give me something. But I'm going to need something from you to sweeten the deal for my company. Can you give me something to trade for you?" I may not be happy, but at least it looks like the salesperson was going out of his or her way to try to make something happen.

Then I won't feel so bad when you come back and tell me, "Well, Steve, I fought for you, even put my career on the line, and I convinced my manager to play ball because you are such an important customer. At first, he actually wanted to pull the deal off the table, but I convinced him to give you a 2-percent discount in return for a small increase in the parts and labor."

Sounds corny, I know, but it is better than telling a tough customer, "No problem, we can do that," and losing valuable ground or denying me any concession because "your manager won't let you." When up against someone who plays hardball, each and every concession must be positioned as a potential deal breaker.

About now, you may be asking yourself, "Isn't this a game?" And the answer is yes. This is a game. It sounds like a game because it is a game. However, it's a tough negotiator's game and they play it well. Does it work? Yes. The alternative is to walk away from a sale or take a deal that makes less and less sense for your company.

To this end, I use phrases like:

"Wow, that's a lot to ask. I'm not sure we have enough margin in our pricing to accommodate your request."

"We might be able to do that for you, but not at *that* price."

"You're not serious, are you?"

"Well, we can do anything you want. But not for free."

And, of course, the corny but useful phrase "You're killing me here!"

These may sound contrived until you realize how easily the other side uses the same phrases. Tough customers will lie (embellish) and bluff (make idle threats) to get you to give ground. Remember the car dealer's definition of the toughest customer: "No matter how much of a deal you give them, they're never satisfied." It should be the same with you when up against a tough negotiator.

Even when you think the concession is a long shot, don't be afraid to initiate the request for a concession to throw the other side off balance. I worked with a software design firm that almost always requested exclusivity at the beginning of their negotiations; they rarely got it, but they always asked for it. And they used the denial from the customer as a leverage point in the negotiation.

"Well, we could have given you that price, but only if we had the exclusive rights to your process. But since you can't give that to us, we will have to say no to your request."

Now, you may be asking yourself whether these tactics border on unethical. Or, to put it another way, "Is it acceptable to lie in a negotiation?"

As a fellow salesperson, I would say no. But the answer to the flipside question, "Will a customer lie to a salesperson to get a better deal?" (yes!) reveals an ethical double standard.

This double-talk has a rationale behind it. Most salespeople and their companies are in the business for the long term and understand the impact that deception can have on credibility and trust. Lying in a negotiation is damaging to a long-term, win-win relationship, something every salesperson values from a customer. Hardball negotiators do not share the same concern; they see products as commodities and agreements as transactions.

Customers get a better deal by treating you and your company as "vendors." They either believe or pretend to believe the relationship is inconsequential. Lying, for them, is a negotiation tactic and is acceptable to increase their "leverage."

So I don't really have a definitive answer to whether lying is an acceptable tactic or a dirty trick. Even some highly ethical negotiators find exaggerating the facts an acceptable tactic. Do you really tell a car dealer how much you have to spend or do you "fudge" a little? Do you really start with your actual budget for a house or do you give yourself room to maneuver?

Here is the answer I came up with to the question of lying in a negotiation: The more important a relationship is to you, the less you should lie.

#2: Never make a concession without getting something in return.

Becoming good at this tactic will significantly improve the profitability of any deal. This is one of the most commonly overlooked negotiation tactics.

Customers, especially tough customers, expect to get concessions without giving up anything in return. They learn this tactic by interacting with salespeople who make concession after concession without demanding reciprocity. Of course, it is also in their best interest to want it all without consequence.

Because of what is at stake, when pressed for a concession, you need to ask yourself three questions. The first is "Do I have to make this concession at all?"

Salespeople often believe they are in a less-powerful position than the customer because they need to sell something. But, you may in fact be in a more powerful position than the customer if the customer's alternatives are not very good.

Of course, tough negotiators seldom let on that they have no intention of giving the business to anyone except you. If you can determine how serious the customer is about denying you the business, you may have enough leverage to refuse their demand. In some cases, your best move might be to refuse to budge any further.

Let's assume, however, you decide that to stay in the game, you need to respond to the demand in some way. The second question to ask yourself is "Can I make a smaller concession than is being demanded?"

If the customer asks for a 5-percent discount, can you offer 2 percent or 3 percent? Never take a demand at face value; take it as an opening position. The other side can always refuse. And if they do, at least you set a precedent for future concession requests.

The third, most important, and most-often-neglected question to ask yourself is: "If I give this up, what do I get in return?" The key to ensuring your most profitable outcome is setting the expectation that you will not give up something that has a financial impact on your organization without demanding something in return.

Let me illustrate by using a typical negotiation dialogue. The customer says to you, "Well, I think we can complete this deal if you can get us another 5-percent discount."

Wrong response: "Sure, we can do that."

Another wrong response: "My manager won't let me do that."

Still another wrong response: "Guess I won't make my quota this month."

Better response: "You're killing me here! This deal is already cutting our margin pretty thin. If we can close this deal today, I can get you a 2-percent discount, but *only* if we can get the purchase order opened today."

Much better response: "Man, you're killing me here! Our margins are cut to the bone. But I will tell you what I am going to do. If we can close this deal today and get the purchase order opened, I can give you a 1.75-percent discount on the up-front costs if you are willing to cover the shipping charges. How does that sound?"

To become a better negotiator against tough customers, you have to get good at playing their game.

#3: Trade the things that cost you the least and have the most value for the other side.

I recently spent a day working with a new client, a major insurance company in Nebraska. After strategizing in a conference room for most of the day, we all decided that a nice dinner and drinks would be a good end to our work. We ended up dining at a well-known and fairly expensive steak house in the local area. Upon receiving the check after dinner, one of the executives said coyly, "Hey Steve. How about we negotiate who is going to pick up the bill for dinner?"

He was obviously feeling confident after having spent the day talking negotiation strategy with me and his team.

"No need to negotiate; I'll gladly pay for our dinner," I said.

Looking a bit flabbergasted he said, "But I thought one of your principles was holding your ground. That didn't seem like you tried very hard. I thought you told us never to fold like that!"

I responded, "Yes, but you didn't let me finish. Remember that one of my other key principles is making sure you get something in return. So I will pick up dinner if you will do something for me."

"Okay, what do you want in return for covering the check?"

"I will pick up dinner if you will send an e-mail to the executives of the other 49 states recommending my services. And I'd also like to be copied on the e-mail."

The executive picked up the check and looked at the total charge again. "I think we have a deal," he said.

So I paid a restaurant tab of more than $500 for an introduction to a group of decision-makers that to date has turned into more than $200,000 in additional business. I try to schedule a dinner with all my clients after spending a day with them.

And I always expect them to want to "negotiate" the bill.

For some reason, salespeople like to think in whole numbers. They will concede in 5, 10, and even 15 percentage-point increments. But ask yourself, if the customer wants a 5-percent reduction, can you get the same result with a 1.5-percent or 1.35-percent reduction? Never give the customer exactly the amount they are demanding. That sets the negotiating bar very low for you and begs the other side to ask for more.

Once you determine the things that are in play, protect the things that cost you and your company the most. Again, if you can get a sale at list price and a "free lunch," take the client to lunch. Salespeople often make the mistake of trying to get the customer to "bite" by offering larger concessions than are necessary. The key to success is to get the most ground with the least amount of give away by hard selling each concession.

Price is the most quantifiable part of a negotiation and often the most expensive to give up. But many terms and conditions have a high cost as well. Post-sales support and service, generous payment terms, delivery charges; these things can erode the profitability of a deal even while maintaining your "price."

That is not to say you don't trade them for things you and your side might want or need, but be careful. As a former sales manager, I found it very frustrating when my people gave away valuable add-ons just to "sweeten" the deal. Most times, even with some "sweetener" added, we didn't get the business. I believe this was, most likely, because the deal was based on price, not value.

If you can move the deal forward by offering something of little cost to your side, then do it. And sometimes it pays to let the other side quantify the value of a concession instead of you. If you can get them to quantify the concession value using the question "Well, how much do you think this is worth?" it can get you more than you anticipated.

My older daughter, Alexis, was flying home from school a couple of winters ago; she was scheduled to arrive three days before Christmas. The airline, which I will not name, ran out of deicing fluid and their flights were cancelled for days. (I found this strange, as many of their flights are to Alaska and Northern Canada.)

After many tears of frustration dealing with the airline's customer service department, she was able to finally get a flight home arriving on Christmas Eve. So after her much-shortened holiday, I called the airline's customer service department to negotiate some sort of recompense.

As I explained the situation to the customer service agent, the company pulled out the usual excuses, which of course I needed to deflect.

"Mr. Reilly, with all due respect, no one could have predicted a storm lasting that long in Seattle."

"Actually, that isn't true. This storm was fore-casted for at least a week. Your company could have planned better."

Another challenge: "Yes, but the snow affected all our flights around the country. We had no way to get her home."

"Actually, you could have put her on another airline since it was your mistake. They continued to fly in and out of Seattle. The ticketing agent refused to do that for her."

And on and on this conversation went.

Finally, in a frustrated tone she asked me, "What would you like me to do, Mr. Reilly?"

"I think you and your airline should figure that out. What is my daughter missing two days with her family worth?"

"I don't know, Mr. Reilly. What would you have us do?"

"Well, what do you think is the right thing?"

(At this point, my daughter, who was listening to the exchange from her bedroom, shouted "Ask them for a pony!" Hilarious! What a great tension-breaker, but I didn't.)

In exasperation, the customer service agent said, "Mr. Reilly, would it be acceptable to you if we refunded the price of the ticket?"

"That would make me happy—and can you also send me some first-class upgrade coupons for the inconvenience?" My response was more a statement than a question.

"I think we can do that."

And everyone was happy. No, scratch that—I was happy. So if the customer values the item you are conceding, it isn't a bad idea to put them on the spot by asking, "Well, what would something like that be worth to you?"

I expected the airline to offer a small concession, like a drink coupon or something of lesser value than the price of the ticket. When the customer service agent offered more than I expected, though, I was pleasantly surprised. I still asked for more, because it never hurts, but I was still surprised.

Had I initially suggested a first-class voucher, I would have negotiated away a whole airline ticket without even realizing it. Though the situation worked out well for me, the airline's customer service representative committed our cardinal sin: She gave away something for nothing. She could have said, "The next two times you fly with us, we'll give you first-class upgrades."

In doing this, she would have appeased me and ensured my future business instead of simply giving me a refund without securing anything in return. This is one of many examples I witness in which companies and salespeople give precious ground instead of trading it for something of equal or better value.

Ask and then wait; be prepared to play the waiting game. Even if at first the other side doesn't have a good response, give them time. They'll come up with something. You might be surprised. I was.

Consider this classic example. A customer says, "I don't know if we are going to make this deal work unless you throw in shipping costs, a 2-percent price reduction, and cover our startup costs with some sort of discount."

The salesperson replies, "Well, I don't know if we can do that. I'll have to talk to my manager and see if I can get approval." The next day, after talking with his manager, the salesperson calls the customer and tells him, "Well, my manager won't let me we do anything on the price, but we are willing to cover the shipping costs. Will that work for you?"

Sound familiar?

This is a typical example of giving too much ground without getting anything in return. At least in this situation the salesperson avoided giving the customer everything he requested; he may have given ground in smaller increments than the customer wanted, but he still made the mistake of not asking for anything in return.

Another favored trick of tough negotiators is getting you to negotiate with yourself. They do this by refusing your original offer as unreasonable and using annoying figures of speech like "These numbers are not going to work. Can you go back and sharpen your pencil and resubmit?"

If you respond by doing as the buyer asks, you are negotiating against yourself. This is a tough negotiation tactic and seems like cheating, but it works. Clients submit re-priced proposals just to get the customer's attention without asking for an idea of how far off their numbers are. Negotiating against yourself sets a very bad negotiation precedent.

The best response to this type of tactic is to insist that the customer give you some idea of how "off" your numbers are. Respond with something like "Well, before I revisit my numbers, can you give me an idea of how far off they are?" or "I'm sorry, but you'll have to be more specific. I can't simply go back and redo my numbers without something to work with."

Be persistent. Buyers will wait you out by not responding to your e-mails or voice mails or will simply send an e-mail asking for a revised bid. Resist the urge to re-bid just to get their attention.

Now, if your conscience and risk tolerance will let you use the same technique with the buyer, then go for it. Telling a buyer that his request is unreasonable might work. You will never know until you try.

#4: Challenge every counteroffer.

As the saying goes, "Once an offer is on the table, the next person who speaks loses." Although silence can be an effective tactic in some negotiation situations, challenging a counteroffer is much more effective.

It is a mistake to think that once the trading begins, you are done testing the other side's numbers. Typically, the process evolves into an offer–counteroffer; offer–counteroffer; and on and on. But holding your ground is about challenging every counter, again and again. Make it tough on tough negotiators. They are not used to having their counters challenged, and it makes it more difficult for them to go on the offensive.

Let's go back to the Kinko's story and Greg for an example of how to challenge counteroffers to get a better deal.

Greg says to me, "So Mr. Reilly, we aren't able to give you the volume discount you requested, but we are able to offer you a 20-percent discount on your next order."

Challenging the Countering Process

First Offer		First Counter
Second Counter	challenge → ←	Third Counter
Fourth Counter	challenge → ←	Fifth Counter
Etc.	challenge → ←	Etc.

I would challenge that with something like "Where did you get the 20 percent on the next order figure?"

Greg might respond, "What do you mean?"

"Well, you are offering me a 20-percent discount on my next order. How about 10 percent on this order and 10 percent on the next? It is the same thing, really."

And Greg responds, "Well, I guess so . . . ."

Challenging counteroffers is very similar to challenging opening positions, so of course the questions are similar:

"How did you arrive at that number?"

"How did you come up with that counter?"

"Why is it so important you get XYZ?"

"How much flexibility do you have with this counteroffer?"

"Is this counteroffer firm, negotiable, or O.B.O.?"

Just as you can challenge their counteroffer, expect that they will challenge yours. So the questions you need to be prepared for when countering are "How did you arrive at that counter?" and "What makes that fair?" Make sure you can defend your counteroffer with a logical argument and strong value proposition. This communicates that you will remain a worthy opponent throughout the entire negotiation.

From here, the process becomes iterative: offer–challenge–counteroffer–challenge, and so forth. Both sides grind away at each other until one side runs out of room to maneuver. At that point, the negotiation moves into its end stage. Now is the time for a Best and Final Offer.

FOUR

Best and Final Offer

Closing the Deal

"Is that your best and final offer?" the chief sourcing officer asked.

My client, an aerospace company, and I were trying to close a deal with an offshore manufacturer of an important mainframe component after six months of hardball negotiations. After some initial grandstanding and positioning, both my client and the manufacturer had settled into a comfortable but wary negotiating environment. By this point, both sides had given quite a bit of ground in a process that included three counteroffers and multiple meetings. Most of the line items had been agreed upon, but there were still some outstanding issues regarding delivery, post-sale service, and support. In spite of that, the manufacturer did not understand what he was asking for in this particular phase of the negotiation.

I wanted to be sure before we answered.

"Are you asking for our best and final offer?" I asked.

"Yes, I am asking if this is the best you can do," he countered.

"Perhaps you don't realize what you are asking," I said.

"I think I do. I'm asking whether or not this is your best and final offer. Seems pretty clear to me."

"Yes, but a best and final offer is a pretty serious request. Don't you think?"

"Not really. You give us your best shot and we will then give you our best shot," he answered testily.

"Well then, that's not a best and final," I said.

"What do you mean?"

"I mean that if we present you our best and final offer, we will then be asking you to take it or leave it; to decide to take our final contract design and sign it or find another vendor."

"No, no. That's not a best and final offer. A best and final offer is your last, best price. Then we counter that and see if we can reach an agreement," he said confidently.

"That's not the way we work. If you want our best and final offer, then the only choice you have is to either take it or walk away. That is why they call it a 'best and final offer,'" I said.

Clearly frustrated, he stepped back a minute.

"Okay, then maybe we aren't ready for your best and final at this point. So this is just a counteroffer that is on the table, right?" he asked.

"Yes. But if you'd like us to take this back and rework it as a best and final offer, we can do that."

"No, no. I don't think we've reached that point yet."

"I agree."

Best and Final Offer Strategy

One of the trickiest and most important parts of negotiating is holding the ground you've spent time and effort protecting as you try to bring a deal to a close. Depending on how well you've defended your price, you may or may not have a good deal at this point. But even if you've held your ground and carved out a good deal, a tough customer will try to "nibble" away until you end up with a less-profitable deal than you thought. Good negotiators will wear you down;

it's part of their strategy. A negotiation can be a long process, and you have to resist the urge to give in due to impatience, irritation, or exhaustion.

Sometimes it seems as though the counter-offering process could go on forever with smaller and smaller concessions from each side. But at some point, one side or the other runs out of room to maneuver and it is time to bring the negotiation to a close. This is a tricky and sometimes fatal phase, if poorly navigated.

It is my experience that there is one common mis-conception about the idea of making a Best and Final Offer. I work in many industries in which proposing multiple Best and Final Offers is standard procedure. The reason it becomes common to make multiple Best and Final Offers in some businesses is mostly because negotiators accept counters even once the final offer is made. When done often enough, this becomes standard operating procedure.

Even though one side will use the term, they actu-ally do not consider it the end of the negotiation; they may consider it an end-phase, but they surely don't use the term as it is intended. However, in some industries, like the heavy equipment market, a Best and Final Offer is always best and final.

A Best and Final Offer, when used as it should, is the final move in negotiation and is intended to bring the counteroffering process to a close. Once the countering process has exhausted the room of one side or the other to maneuver, a Best and Final is intended to bring the negotiation to its conclusion. There is no counteroffer to a Best and Final Offer; there is only a thumbs up or thumbs down. So proposing a true Best and Final Offer is a pretty serious matter. You need to make sure you are serious about it.

The party that makes the final offer is asking the other side to either accept or reject the terms and conditions of that offer, with no counteroffer. This means that if you are the party that makes the Best and Final Offer, you should be prepared to walk away from the negotiation if the other side rejects it. That is how it is supposed to work, in theory. Reality, however, is more complex.

There are three important interrelated characteristics that come into focus when you reach the endgame in a negotiation: your bottom line, your walk-away option(s), and leverage. To be successful at any negotiation, it is important to understand the interplay among these three factors. Knowing how to use these factors becomes especially important when up against tough customers.

Let's start with definitions. This is going to come at you fast, so pay attention.

Your bottom line is the worst deal you will accept. If you can't get a price better than your bottom line, then you might be better off not doing the deal. When you decide you aren't going to reach a deal, then you walk away. A bottom line triggers the use of your walk-away option.

Your walk-away option is what you will do if negotiations break down; it is another option or options you might consider other than continuing to bargain to reach a deal. If you decide to walk away from any potential deal, then the negotiation is over. This is, of course, unless you are using the threat of walking away as a tactic to get a better deal. In any negotiation, whether it is simple or complex, the better your walk-away option, the more leverage you typically have; remember that I said "typically." The negotiating party that has the most options, whether they are other competing offers, no real need to make a deal, or can just simply walk away from the negotiation with no consequences, can have the most leverage.

The interplay among these three factors can seem confusing and difficult to use in negotiation so we need to understand how they affect each other.

Let's start with bottom line.

Bottom Line

One of the most important of pieces of a negotiation strategy is the concept of a "bottom line." A bottom line is the worst deal you will accept in any given negotiation. It isn't a good deal at all. Reaching a deal that is the same as your bottom line is not success; it is definitely less than success, but at least you have a deal.

Even before thinking about your walk-away option, identifying your bottom line is a key step to success.

To ensure we understand how a bottom line is used, let's come back to the used car example. (Once again, I apologize for using such a threadbare and overused analogy, but it is easy to understand.)

As we talked about earlier in the book, you've decided to list your car on Craigslist, eBay, Auto Trader, or some other Website for $17,000. Then, prior to listing it, you decide for whatever reason that you will not accept anything less than $12,500. In other words, if you get any offers at $12,499 or less, you will reject them. This makes $12,500 your bottom line.

Now, based on the response or lack of response to your ad, you may need to rethink your bottom line; but you get the idea. Having a bottom line as a trigger to walking away can keep you from being taken advantage of, from agreeing to something that doesn't "make sense" to you—sometimes.

That said, many salespeople I work with complain that their companies take deals that "don't make sense." What that means is that the deal doesn't make sense at their level, perhaps not from a dollars and cents perspective, but it may make sense from another perspective. For instance, I have many clients that will lose money on a deal in order to gain market share; that's called a penetration strategy. I have other clients who will make a deal that loses money to get a "name" customer to improve their brand. And although an individual salesperson may not think it makes sense, senior management might. If pushed enough, though, you might decide to sell the car for less than your bottom line ($12,500), perhaps because you might need the money for some emergency or some other legitimate reason.

A factor that can often ruin a negotiation is a bottom line that is too inflexible. Saying something like

"I would never accept less than . . ." is not in your best interest when negotiating. A rigid bottom line can become a hindrance to reaching a deal. The phrase "I would never . . . !" can sabotage negotiations and keep a party from reaching an agreement that might be in their best interest.

The best use of a bottom line is as a guideline, not a rule. Let me explain.

I am involved in negotiations all the time in which my clients have to rethink their bottom line. Just like in the example of selling your car, if you cannot sell it for $12,500 or better, and are unwilling to walk away (take it off the market), then you need to reset your expectations regarding the bottom line you've set. And because your bottom line ($12,500) was the worst deal that you would accept, you may feel forced into taking a bad deal and accept an offer less than your bottom line because you don't have any choice; you don't have any better alternatives.

That happens all the time, especially these days.

Since the recent bursting of the housing bubble, many homeowners are in the position that their bottom line, or worst offer they will or can accept, is lower than the amount they owe on their homes. So many cannot even entertain offers lower than the amount of their outstanding mortgage. This limits their walk-away options, which weakens their leverage.

This is a very unfortunate and unpleasant situation to be in, especially if this seemed unfathomable when you qualified for a mortgage based on an inflated house value. Unfortunately for many of them, they cannot or will not simply walk away. In the case of those homeowners who have been able to sell their homes, many were forced to sell below the bottom line they held at the beginning of the sales process.

But let's use a slightly more-complex situation to help grasp these highly theoretical concepts.

In a hospital-insurer negotiation, prior to opening discussions, both sides will try and figure out their bottom lines, or the worst deal they will accept. If you had the opportunity to compare each side's bottom lines before any counteroffers, you would find that, though still different, they would most likely be closer to each other than would be each side's first offer—that the gap at the beginning of the negotiation was wider than at the end of the negotiation.

These are often closer than their first offer, but still quite far apart. (I know because I consult to both sides of the industry.) So if you think about it, they will never reach agreement unless one side or the other, or both, rethink their bottom line. In complex negotiations, bottom lines are fungible and malleable. So it is best to consider your bottom line as a guideline, not a firm number. I have seen many negotiations that start with a firm bottom line only to see that number rise and fall based on other considerations.

This is how it goes. An insurer starts with an opening offer of an increase of 5 percent over the previous years' reimbursement. Then let's say that the insurer has determined that it will not go above an 8-percent increase (bottom line), no matter the situation.

That may be a good intention, but as the offer and counteroffers fly, the insurer may realize (just as you did in the used car negotiation) that 5 percent was unrealistic based on the information gained in the negotiation itself. They may even realize that by going higher than 8 percent, but getting serious and important reciprocal counter concessions, that it is actually in their "interest" to offer a higher reimbursement, providing they get substantial concessions in return.

When dealing with tough customers, you can quickly end up closer to your bottom line than you might in a more collaborative negotiation. Tough negotiators will push you as far as they can; they want you to give up all the wiggle room you have, all the way down to your bottom line. And though you may use your bottom line as a measure of success, you can be sure that they measure their negotiation success by how close the end result is to their first offer. You should, too.

Comparing your first offer to the final deal gives you a standard with which to measure your success with time. The closer you end up to your first offer, the better you did as a negotiator.

To illustrate how a non-negotiable bottom line can sometimes interfere with getting the best deal, here is a scenario that I recently experienced in my own negotiation over a new car.

Now, as a negotiation consultant, there are some things I would consider non-negotiable, right? There are lines that I would never cross because they just seem so basic and straightforward. One line that I had up until recently was that I would never pay full sticker price for a car. Being fluent in all these negotiation skills makes me pretty confident that I can get the best deal by grinding the car dealership down to a significant discount.

In most negotiation situations, I set my bottom line or minimum amount of a discount I would accept at 10 percent. But recently, I was in the market for a new business auto and went about the process of acquiring a new set of wheels. After visiting a number of dealerships and negotiating a number of significant discounts, I happened to visit my local dealer one last time before making a deal.

Because I already had more than one excellent deal on the table from each dealer, I felt safe enough to lay all my cards on the table, providing the salesperson with terms and conditions of the various deals I had negotiated with competing dealerships. I then told him that if his dealership could do better than any of those I already had on the table, I might consider it. If not, then I would close the deal with the other dealership with the best discount.

His first question threw me, at first.

"So how do you typically do on your investments? What is your average rate of return?"

"What do you mean, my investments?" I asked.

"Yes. Do you know your typical yearly return rate for your retirement funds or anything like that?"

Being in business for myself, I pay very good attention to my investment returns.

I answered, "I do pretty well. Last year was a particularly good year and I think I ended up at about an overall return of 12 percent."

The salesperson paused then asked, "When you showed me the deals you negotiated with the other car dealers, the common thing I see is that the better the offer, the higher your down payment."

"Yes, that's right. Putting some skin in the game gave me more leverage."

"So do you just keep all that cash on hand?" he asked.

"Of course not, but I have some pretty liquid investments to draw from." And I added, very cocksure, "Don't worry. I have the money."

He very politely pounced, "Yes, but tying all that money up in a depreciating asset doesn't seem to make sense from an investment standpoint."

"I don't really see what you are getting at," I said, now getting a bit put off by his cocksure attitude.

"Well, if you took the money you plan to use as a down payment and invested it, even at a conservative 5-percent return, that would be better than putting it into an asset that loses value each day you drive it," he said.

"Yes, but you can see the substantial discounts I've negotiated and I expect to finance the balance with a short-term loan from my bank."

"But what if you didn't have to put a down payment on the car and could get a no-interest loan?"

"What's the catch?" I asked. I'd been at this too long to assume there wasn't one.

"The only catch is that to get this offer you have to pay full price for the car."

"You mean the sticker price?"

"Yes, it is the only way we can make any money on this type of deal. It is a one-time offer to get rid of last year's models before the new styles come out."

As it happened, the dealership was having a special financing offer of 0-percent down with 0 interest for the life of the loan. It was an end-of-the-year special and the dealer was motivated to deplete his stock prior to receiving the new year models and styles. The one non-negotiable point was that the deal was only available to a buyer who paid full sticker price.

Not fully understanding the financial complexity behind this offer, I called my accountant. I needed some guidance regarding the financial/tax incentives laid out in the dealer's proposal. I couldn't figure out whether this deal was better than the negotiated discounts with the other dealers. So I explained the offer of zero down with zero financing.

He asked me, "Is this the car you want?"

"Yes, I've narrowed my search down to this make and model."

He said without hesitation, "Then take the deal."

"Are you sure?" I asked.

"Absolutely. This is by far the best deal for you."

"Really? Even though I have to pay full sticker price?"

"Even if you have to pay full sticker price. It's the best deal."

As he had never steered me wrong in the 20 years I've worked with him, I took the deal.

Later, my accountant explained the time value of money in this situation. He said that for every month of the loan payment, the price of the car actually fell. He said that the longer the payment plan, the less money the car cost. He told me to get the loan for the longest payback period the dealer would allow and keep my money where it was.

When he showed me the math, with the assumption of a 2-percent increase in inflation, I quickly realized that it didn't make sense to acquire this car any other way. When you added the increase of the value of the dollar due to inflation over the life of the interest-free loan, I was coming out way ahead of all the other deals. The savings I incurred by paying full sticker price with a no-interest loan, far exceeded any discount I had already negotiated with other dealers. It was clear that paying full sticker price with no down payment and 0-percent financing was actually in my best interest.

So at the beginning of my car shopping expedition, the bottom line I had in my head was getting at least a 10-percent discount off sticker price (first offer). But with new information and a bit of quick calculations, it became very clear that I needed to change—even disregard—my original bottom line.

Never say never, as they say.

Walk-Away Option

Walking away is terminating the negotiation altogether. It is breaking off discussions and moving on. Your walk-away option is the action or actions you will take to satisfy your interests if in fact you cannot reach an agreement—if you cannot reach a deal that "makes sense." Using the used car scenario, we used $12,500 as the original bottom line. If, again, you are truly serious about holding to your bottom line and receive no offers at or better than the $12,500 number, then one option is to donate the car. Another option is to use it as a trade-in on a new car or, if it is fully insured, leave it in the airport parking lot with the engine running and keys in it (a joke). Using the example of selling a house, if you only receive offers well below your asking price or no offers at all, one option is to convert the home into a rental unit. Another might be to use it as an Airbnb, or perhaps remodel it and place it back on the market at a later date. Still another is, if the home is fully insured . . . again, a joke.

This brings us to the concept of BATNA. Remember that? Best Alternative to a Negotiated Agreement, or BATNA, is a fancy acronym for the rather simple idea of using your walk-away option. A walk-away option is what you will do if you can't reach an agreement; it is an alternative to continuing to bargain and attempting to reach a deal. When you take your BATNA, or walk-away option, you are cutting off any further negotiation with your opponent: no more counteroffers, no more haggling over the price; you are done negotiating and acccpt that

The Used Car Example

Negotiation		
	$17,000	Your Asking Price
	$4,500	Wiggle Room
	$12,500	Your Bottom Line
	>$12,500 Lower than your Bottom Line	Walk-Away Option • Use as trade-in • Donate • Continue to drive

you will never reach an agreement on this particular negotiation with this particular person or entity, ever.

According to Ury and Fisher, you can walk away from any negotiation. The authors purport that by having a good walk-away option (BATNA), you protect yourself from difficult opponents. They advocate walking away from more powerful opponents so you don't give away the store, or at the very least, take a deal that doesn't "make sense."

In theory, this might work, but in the world of selling, it is folly.

Telling a salesperson to walk away from the negotiation table and kissing off a sale is a bit cavalier for an expert who's never had to make a living by making a quota. For those of us who have spent a significant portion of our careers in sales, we know we would never just up and walk away from a potential sale, no matter how slim the chances are of actually getting the business. That is one of the characteristics that makes salespeople successful: irrational optimism in the face of certain defeat.

Technically, you might have the ability to abort negotiations on a big deal, but you still have a quota to make and a job to keep.

With that said, however, salespeople are *always* better negotiators when they've already reached their quota. Why? Because they don't need the business. Still, they may indeed walk away from a particular negotiation, but they always come back as the situation changes.

As a sales manager, I urged my team to have as many potential prospects as possible. I encouraged them to be working on many potential deals, not just because it would help them make quota, but also because it made them tougher negotiators. They were all much better at holding their ground when they didn't feel desperate to have a customer's business.

(For those fellow sales managers out there: Do you know what the number-one indicator is of how well a salesperson knows his or her business? Give up? The answer is forecasting accuracy. The better salespeople know their business, the better their forecast. You're welcome.)

Here's an important side note:

At times, I get the opportunity to discuss the skills taught in the *Getting to Yes* seminar with people who attended the workshop in the past. I always ask them, "What is the thing you most remember about the Ury and Fisher approach?" to which I receive the almost universal response: "The thing I remember most is to make sure you know your BATNA."

Even though most cannot recall what the initials stand for, they believe that knowing which options they have if negotiations break down empowers them a bit. I find it curious that the term most remembered from a course designed specifically to improve negotiation skills is one that describes how to walk away from the table—in other words, by refusing to negotiate.

Go figure.

Keep in mind, though, that your customer or the other side of the table also has a walk-away option. The difference between their walk-away option and your walk-away option is called leverage.

Leverage

Leverage is the ability to influence the decisions and actions of your opponent. When you use leverage, you are really trying to get the other side to give in or make a concession. Leverage is an important part of any negotiation, and it can come in many forms. In situations in which you have good walk-away options, you usually have the upper hand. In situations in which your walk-away option sucks, the other side has the upper hand. The more leverage you have, the more likely you are to reach an agreement that best meets your goals in any negotiation.

There are three different leverage positions.

First Leverage Position

The first is when your walk-away options are better than the other side's walk-away options. In this situation, you have the upper hand and can usually translate that into a better deal for your side. You then have more leverage. You are usually in the driver's seat in this case.

Try to determine who has the most leverage in this situation:

I buy almost all of my technology items off Craigslist. Now for those of you who immediately dismiss me as a nut, let me explain. When I am in the market for a new iPhone or MacBook, the first place I search is on Craigslist. Although the latest release phone or computer is often not available, or at least not available at a significant discount, there is always a plethora of late model phone and computers to choose from available on the Website.

I always search for sellers in my hometown, Seattle (there have been so many scams on selling Websites, so I only do face-to-face transactions). When it comes to a MacBook, I look for a good-condition model with all the software and updates I use on a regular basis. This can save me quite a bit of money, as Microsoft Office, Adobe Acrobat, and other applications can add hundreds of dollars to any store-bought computer.

I then arrange to meet the seller at a local coffee shop (not difficult to find, especially in Seattle. There is one at the end of everyone's driveway—almost). Meeting in a safe, well-lit, and crowded venue eliminates the chance of being scammed or robbed. When the seller and I connect, I have them run the device through its paces to ensure everything works. I then have the person wipe the hard drive clean of all their files, except for the software.

So think about walk-away options for both myself and the seller. At this point, the seller has taken the time to drive to meet me, run the device through its paces, and discuss the life of the computer. Now ask yourself, "Who has the better walk-away option: the seller or me?"

For me, I don't even have to leave the coffee shop to find another computer or phone simply by using the Craigslist app. The seller, however, has to wait for another potential buyer to contact them and then arrange a sale. This gives me the most leverage. Whether you use it or not to offer less at this point is up to you. Even if I don't use this leverage, I know that I am in the stronger negotiating position.

But sometimes, even when salespeople are in a strong negotiating position, they still give ground unnecessarily.

I have a client who makes the world's only infectious disease test on the market, with the highest accuracy and shortest time to result. It saves time, money, effort, and, most importantly, lives. They have an exclusive market position with heavy demand from hospitals and physicians. Still, they have salespeople heavily discounting and giving away "free" product. Why?

It isn't because their customers play hardball; they often don't. All they do is ask nicely.

Customers politely ask for a discount and the salespeople accommodate them. Now, I am not saying discounting is always bad. I am saying that if a salesperson discounts and receives nothing in return, he or she could do a better job of negotiating.

I share this story to help you understand that good negotiation strategy isn't simply knowing your walk-away options; it is also knowing your opponent's walk-away options. Tough customers will make threats that have no substance to see if you flinch, to see if they can eke out a little more profit for themselves.

Second Leverage Position

The second leverage situation is when the other side has the better walk-away option and, thus, the upper hand. In this situation, the other side can use its leverage to get a better deal for their side. This can put you at a disadvantage if you aren't familiar with techniques for eroding their leverage, but we will get to that.

Consider the case of the current housing market. As of this writing, housing in my hometown is a "sellers" market. This means that the seller is in a better negotiation position than is the buyer. This gives the seller the upper hand, and so houses are selling at their listing price or above. The seller then has more leverage than the buyer.

This is often the case in commodity markets in which differentiation is difficult and there is parity among suppliers. But remember, although that might put you in a poor negotiation position, you still can trade concessions to prevent being taken unfair advantage of.

Most salespeople believe they are in this position more often than not. Because they have to seek out potential customers and not the other way around, they often feel as though they are at the mercy of the buyer and, therefore, need to discount to get the business. This is not always the case.

Third Leverage Position: The "Nuclear Option"

The third and last leverage position is sometimes referred to as the "nuclear option." This is the negotiation situation in which neither side can afford to walk away from the negotiation because the damage done to each would be far more painful than working through to an acceptable agreement.

In the aviation industry, it is common for a company like Boeing to use a sole-source supplier for a critical part like an aircraft wing or fuselage. In a situation like this, Boeing is as equally reliant on the customer as the customer is on Boeing. The supplier is then a business-critical link in the supply chain and Boeing is a customer the supplier cannot afford to lose. Sometimes referred to as an interdependent or symbiotic relationship, it is important for both parties to realize the interdependency and work toward win-win solutions. Playing hardball in these situations can do long-term damage to relationships, especially in matters of trust. That is one of the reasons sole-source contracts are so difficult to negotiate; it often leaves one or both parties in a vulnerable position.

Perhaps this book isn't as applicable to the "nuclear option" leverage position except for the idea that, if you are in one of those interdependent business relationships, you should avoid making threats.

There Is No Fourth Leverage Position

I am sometimes asked if there is a fourth situation with regard to leverage. Using the same logic, the person points out that there might be a situation in which both sides have a good walk-away option. The thinking goes that if both sides can walk away from a negotiation, then each have very powerful positions and therefore cancel out each other's leverage, just like two negotiators who both have poor walk-away options. This seems logical in theory, but in the real world it really doesn't make sense. Why would either party put up with hardball bargaining if they could simply walk away and get a better deal from someone else? It's like a person with a car who has lots of full price offers negotiating with a person who doesn't need a car. It doesn't make sense.

Real Leverage and Faux Leverage

A couple of years ago, I was involved in a negotiation situation in Seattle between my client, a major health insurer, and one of the city's largest hospital chains. I was asked to provide some guidance when the hospital chain began making unreasonable demands. Among other egregious demands, the hospital administrator was asking the insurer for increases to reimbursement rates that were simply not sustainable in the competitive Seattle market. After months of haggling and distrust between the two parties, they were at loggerheads with time running out on the agreement for the following year. Still, the increases demanded by the hospital administrator were so large that the insurer would have had to lose money for a number of years before it would begin to make a profit.

Again and again, the hospital system administrators threatened to go "non-par," or non-participating, in which all of their facilities would become "out-of-network" for thousands of employees in the greater Northwest. These employees would either have to find new doctors and new hospitals or pay the hefty out-of-network bills issued by the hospital. The hospital even engaged a public relations firm to place newspaper articles describing my client as "the worst" bad-faith negotiator in the insurance market and "difficult to do business with."

In frustration and desperation, my client decided to call the hospital administrator's bluff. They made a Best and Final Offer to the hospital, which was immediately rejected by the administrator.

In the final meeting between the two parties, my client then told the hospital to go ahead and begin communicating the anticipated disruption in the network to their patients via a "term letter" to all patients and providers. (This is required by law in most states if a hospital and insurer cannot reach agreement.) The hospital system administrator stormed out of the meeting, threatening to sue the insurer and "put them out of business" in the state of Washington.

A week later, the chastised and chagrined hospital administrator asked if he could secretly meet with my client to see if they couldn't work out a deal that might be amenable to both sides. In a rare and final demonstration of audacity, the administrator said they would accept the terms and conditions of the last offer (Best and Final Offer) by my client.

Against my recommendation, and in spite of having the upper hand by calling the hospital's bluff, the insurer agreed to the offer that had been left on the table prior to the disruption by the hospital walking away from negotiations, but with one additional concession from the hospital. The administrator had to agree to use the same public relations firm to publish an article with the administrator byline (author) stating that the insurer was a trustworthy business partner and focused on the health and welfare of its members. (Care for some great Northwestern microbrew to go with that crow, sir?)

Now it was entirely possible that, instead of calling the hospital system's bluff, my client could have capitulated (caved) and met all of their demands. If that had been the case, then even though the hospital had no intention of following through on the threat, their bluff would have been successful. This is called perceived leverage. And when perceived leverage works, then perceived leverage is leverage. When it doesn't, then it is an idle threat.

When a bluff doesn't work, as was the case in this situation, the hospital was left in a damaged position for this and most likely for negotiations in the near future at least. Idle threats become less and less effective as the other side catches on to the trick.

So the rule of thumb that works best is if you are going to make a threat, be prepared to follow through. Idle threats may work from time to time, but if you get caught it will cost you in the long run.

Here's another negotiation tip: Hospitals mark their patient charges up anywhere from 300 to 3,000 percent. (Yes, you read that correctly.) When presented by a hospital bill, always, always contact the hospital billing department and ask for a significant discount. Most of the time, they will negotiate. If they don't, there is a fast-growing field of consultants called "patient advocates" who will negotiate for you, taking a small percentage of the reduction in charges.

I run into many situations in which a customer is clearly bluffing, but the salesperson folds anyway. I've been in many situations in which a customer threatens to give the business to the competition, even when there is little chance of that happening. Tough customers often attempt to use the threat of walking away as leverage to get a better deal without having any intention of awarding the business to other vendors. They use the tactic against sellers almost without thinking. At times, the bluff can be very obvious.

I had a semi-conductor client who hired me to help reverse the company's margin erosion. Their average sales price was under siege as the salespeople were having a tough time holding the line on price against aggressive customers. This seemed strange to me, especially when the dynamics of this particular market was considered.

My client was confronting downward pressure on prices, even though this particular industry was in the midst of a capacity problem and the market was allocated. At this time, the market for dynamic random access memory, or DRAM, was experiencing a severe shortage of available products due to manufacturing constraints. Because of this, almost all computer manufacturers were "allocated" a specific amount of DRAM chips per month. Their allocated amount of DRAM was always less than they wanted and, so, constrained their ability to make enough product to meet demand. This was the case with every manufacturer and every supplier.

But in spite of this constrained market, my client was seeing significant erosion of its Average Selling Price (ASP). Looking into the problem, I determined that customer sourcing people were threatening to shift the business to other suppliers if my client's salespeople didn't discount their products further. In response, the salespeople almost always gave the customer some sort of discount.

However, when I helped the sales team to think it through, they realized that their buyers were making the idlest of threats. They could threaten all they wanted to switch the business, but they couldn't switch suppliers because other manufacturers had no available product to sell them. Their customers were using a salesperson's natural fear of losing the business to get even deeper discounts. Once the client realized this, they immediately and politely began refusing to discount any products.

Also, at times negotiators get tired of the haggling and the back-and-forth, so they make unnecessary concessions just to "get a deal done." One rule is that the quicker you reach a deal, the more likely that one side left money on the table. Think about it. If you make a first offer and the other side takes it immediately, then you most likely misread the amount of leverage you had in that situation. You probably could have asked for more or offered less. The reverse is true as well. If the other side puts out an unexpectedly attractive offer to you, you could most likely ask for more or offer less and still get a deal.

Keep in mind that the bigger the deal, the longer it should take to complete: the more at stake, the more patient you need to be. Hospital-insurer negotiations take about six months to complete. That seems like a long time. However, if you take into account that a large hospital system can have more than $300 million in reimbursement at risk and the same for an insurer, it should take that long.

Also, especially in a long negotiation, tough customers will "nibble" at the terms and conditions in an attempt to wear you down and force unnecessary concessions. But remember that these nibbles are much less of an issue if you "teach" the other side that you make concessions only in return for reciprocal concessions.

Each time they say, "Oh, and one more little thing . . ." you respond, "Sure we can do that. But not at that price!"

In addition to parrying nibbles from the other side, there are a number of other things you can do to ensure that you hold your ground and, where possible, improve your side of the deal.

Prior to entering into any negotiation, you should determine your bottom line and your alternative strategy if in fact you cannot reach a deal. If you have good options, then you have good leverage. If when selling a car, you get a number of offers but don't sell because you want to maximize your profit, then you have quite a bit of leverage over the next person who makes you an offer because you have many alternatives. However, if the potential buyer has lots of potential sellers, then perhaps your walk-away options cancel each other's out.

In addition to your strategy, you should determine the amount of leverage your opponent has and is willing to use prior to giving your Best and Final Offer. Tough customers will often bluff when, in fact, they have no good alternatives. Their bluster and threats should roll off your back if you know you have the upper hand.

But let's face it, sometimes it's an uphill battle to close the deal and your walk-away options are poor. Even in these cases, though, you are only in a weak negotiation position when two conditions are present.

The first is when the customer has good alternatives: when the product or service is a commodity with many interchangeable, duplicate products in the market. In that situation, the buyer's walk-away is stronger than the seller's. You can try to "sell" them on the uniqueness of your product, but differentiating a commodity is another uphill climb.

The second condition is when the customer knows the salesperson has few options and needs the business—when the buyer knows you need the sale more than he or she needs your product.

The mistake salespeople make when entering the last phase of the negotiation is to believe they are in a weak position because they have to sell something to make a quota and customers don't have to buy something to make a quota. This is especially true for salespeople who are behind in their sales numbers.

They may feel desperate and, because so, in dire need of the business and at the mercy of the customer.

The idea of leverage can get complicated. One reason is because real leverage can change in the middle of negotiating a deal. Let's say you've had your house on the market for a couple of months without receiving any offers. Then you get an offer substantially below your asking price. You don't have much leverage at this point with only two options: Sell at the lower price or wait for another buyer (walk-away option). But let's say that you get another offer around the same price as the first. This gives you more leverage because now you have better options.

Lousy Walk-Away, but a Good Deal

Ultimately, all of the positioning tips and hardball techniques in this book revolve around the following question (and this book's final question): Who has the power in a negotiation? Negotiation experts will tell you that the person with the most power in a negotiation is the one with the ability and nerve to walk away: the customer who has many alternative products and vendors to choose from; the buyer who has multiple approved vendors; the purchasing agent who doesn't need to buy anything. But that answer is too simplistic.

Who has the power in a car negotiation: the buyer or the seller? The answer is the buyer of course—the customer. The customer can always walk out the door; the car dealer has to wait for someone else to walk in the door.

Even though the buyer has better alternatives and the seller has a weak BATNA, most car sellers still get a better deal than most car buyers. Then how do dealers sell their cars with such high-profit margins? The secret is by keeping the customer in the game. A car dealer is a great example of using good negotiation tactics to wear the other side down in spite of being in a weaker negotiating position, thus neutralizing the other side's willingness to walk away and using that leverage to get a good deal.

Why? Here's a quick lesson in negotiation dynamics: The time and effort you put into a negotiation is called "skin in the game." The more skin in the game, the less likely you are to walk. Car dealers know this and use it to their advantage.

Studies by car dealer associations show that the strongest factor in predicting whether or not you will buy a car in a specific dealership on any given day is the length of time you spend in the dealership that day: the hours wasted haggling.

Why the correlation between time spent in the dealership and buying a car? Although those hours may seem wasted to you, they are valuable to the car dealer. Those hours are intended to get you to put more and more "skin" in the game. The longer they keep you, the more skin. The more skin, the less likely you are to walk.

Dealers know this. They know that the more time you spend "haggling," the less likely you are to walk out and subject yourself to the same process at another dealer. Am I suggesting you confine your customers in a small office with bad coffee until they buy? Well, no. This is probably not the best way to win over your customers. But remember that a tough negotiator is patient and will wear you down by keeping you in the game until the very end. Even with poor walk-away alternatives, if you are good at keeping the other side engaged while still holding your ground, you will be a worthy opponent.

The truly powerful negotiator is the one who has few walk-away options, but negotiates a good deal anyway.

Best and Final Offer Tactics

#1: Be the first to ask for their Best and Final Offer.

A good offense is the best defense. At some point it becomes apparent that one side or the other is reaching their limit in terms of room to maneuver—that one side is approaching their bottom line. Figuring out when your opponent is nearing this point can take some skill. A negotiator has to feel the opponent's tension, look for signs of stiffening positions, and intuit when the other side is running out of wiggle room.

For me, or anyone for that matter, to try to tell you how many counteroffers should be on the table before you ask the other side for their Best and Final Offer is not possible. In some industries, multiple counteroffers are standard operating procedure, whereas in others it can be one offer for each side. Of course, in the case of a request for quote (RFQ) or request for proposal (RFP), there is often no opportunity to counteroffer, so you have no opportunity to negotiate (so you better be good at selling). When making a deal with someone on Craigslist or eBay, a single counteroffer is most likely enough to get you a better deal. You wouldn't want to spend the time haggling for very long. Even on Craigslist, that would be more than needed.

Negotiation complexity dictates the number of times you go back and forth to reach a deal. You need a combination of experience and skill. However, just being aware that you want to be the first to ask is a very good start.

There are some other indicators of the timing of your request for a Best and Final Offer.

When good negotiators are forced to give ground, they do so in diminishing increments—smaller and smaller concessions. The first concession you get from a car dealer is most likely the biggest—not the last, but the biggest. They will squeeze the most out of you they can before folding. The closer they are to their bottom line, the tougher it is to wring out additional concessions. This can be an indicator that it is time to put them on the spot by asking for their Best and Final Offer. Pay attention to the value of the concessions as you haggle through the process.

Another way you can get an indication of how close the back-and-forth is getting to its end is by the length of time between offer and counteroffer; typically, the longer the wait, the closer they are to their bottom line. For example, a car dealer will keep you waiting longer and longer between each counteroffer to see if you will throw in the towel and sign on the dotted line; it's part of the game. But two can play that game. If you hang in there long enough, they will often make additional, albeit smaller, concessions.

Remember that tough negotiators try to "keep you in the game" and wring out last-minute concessions. It can become almost a sport for them to push you as close as they can, right up to the point you walk. A car dealer will let you walk to your car before calling to tell you to "come back in and talk about it." Return the favor. Using all your skills and reading their body language, push the other side as far as you think you can. Then ask for their Best and Final Offer before they ask you.

Ending the Countering Process

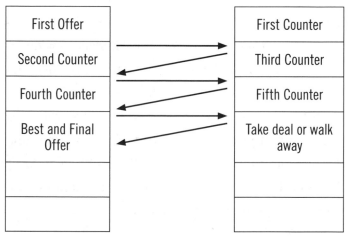

First Offer		First Counter
Second Counter		Third Counter
Fourth Counter		Fifth Counter
Best and Final Offer		Take deal or walk away

#2: Never let anyone counter your Best and Final Offer.

One of the most frequent challenges I encountered as an Instructor of the *Getting to Yes* workshop was how to respond to the question "Is that your Best and Final Offer?" Our scripted response was "When playing win-win, there never is a Best and Final Offer because you always come to a mutually beneficial agreement." Now that sounds good in theory, but in practice there are many situations in which a Best and Final Offer is part of the negotiation process. In binding arbitration and labor negotiations, a Best and Final Offer is legally mandated.

So, what is the best response to the question "Is this your Best and Final Offer?" "Yes" is the wrong answer if it isn't your Best and Final. You only reply in the affirmative if you're willing to lose the deal to a lower price from your competitor. This answer immediately puts you in the position of ending the negotiation if the other side doesn't take your Final Offer.

If you still have room left and want to protect it, "No" is also the wrong response. If you are running out of room to maneuver and tell a tough negotiator that your last offer isn't your Best and Final, prepare yourself for more concessions.

I thought about this for a long time. After I finally figured it out, I realized that I could not have come up with the best response without having been exposed to tough customers and hardball negotiators. Again, I would have never arrived at the best response by simply being exposed to only win-win approaches.

Without having to deal with this question in real-life, down and dirty bargaining, I would have never realized how to respond in a way that both protected me from counters to my Best and Final and allowed for something I might have overlooked as having enough potential value to consider.

The answer I came up with to the question "Is that your Best and Final Offer?" is "This is a good deal and the best we can do. But if you have something else you'd like to throw on the table, we will consider it." Or, another version: "This is the best we can do, but I am willing to negotiate further if you have something else you'd like to discuss."

Both of these responses take the pressure off you to concede further and put it back on the other side to make the next move. If you still have room, these answers also ensure you don't give any more ground without a reciprocal concession. And if it truly is your Best and Final Offer, your response leaves the door open for something you've either overlooked or for an additional concession from the other side that might be in your best interest.

In my experience with using this response, I've been surprised by the number of useful responses received by tough customers. Sometimes they reply with something like, "Well, I don't know. Is there something you want to throw on the table?" To which I might bring up another concession the other side hasn't thought of as a consideration and reopen negotiations.

I am a pretty prolific writer with books on many non-negotiation subjects including leadership, selling, psychology, and philosophy. I also have many friends who always want a "free" copy of my latest book. Before I figured this particular tactic out, I was generous with "absorbing the costs" of these complimentary copies. But what I found was that even though I gave them a "gratis" copy of the book, many did not take the time to read it. Because they had no "skin in the game," there was no pressing need to read the book and so it usually went to the bottom of books already on their reading list.

So I changed my strategy. From then on, I made a deal with them: I was willing to absorb the cost of the book if they would commit to reading it within a month *and* writing a review on my Amazon author

Web page. If I didn't get a review, then I would bill them at a reduced price for the book.

Needless to say, some declined my offer and didn't get a free copy; others gladly read the book within the allotted time and submitted a review to Amazon (almost all were positive reviews, thank goodness).

If you do decide to make a true Best and Final Offer, though, never ever make another concession. A Best and Final Offer means you are willing to lose the deal if the other side turns your offer down. To cough up another concession is to weaken your position in this and future negotiations. If yours is truly a Best and Final Offer and the other side counters, put your stake in the ground: no more concessions. The only acceptable response from the other side is a "thumbs up" or "thumbs down." If you have decided to stand your ground, then accept the consequences.

Also, expect a tough negotiator, in a final attempt to eke out a last concession, to counter with something like "I think we have a deal here. Everything looks great and I am ready to open a purchase order. But my manager now tells me we can't do a deal without an additional 2 percent off the price. I mean, I was just going to open the purchase order and then this. Whaddya say, give me this and we can get things moving before the end of the day?"

Does that sound familiar?

Once again, "You're killing me here!" is your first response. Then, if you feel you have no other choice, you "trade" this final concession for something else. At the minimum, trade it for a signed contract, if not another reciprocal concession. Say something like:

"Sure, I can do something on the price. Let's say you give me the go-ahead to charge for two more training seats and I give you a 1-percent discount. Can you take that back to your boss and see if it flies?"

So, even after a Best and Final Offer is on the table, it might be in your best interest to continue to negotiate if the other side offers something of value. But if they don't, and if you are truly making your Best and Final Offer, the only option for the other side is to take the deal or walk.

#3: Always counter their Best and Final Offer.

Once you've coaxed out their Best and Final Offer, always counter that offer. This may seem obvious enough, but is frequently overlooked as a negotiation tactic. It also seems to go against the previous tactic of not allowing the other side to counter your Best and Final.

When presented with a Best and Final Offer, always ask for "one more thing." This tests their limits and keeps them on the defensive. If they give more ground once they've presented their Best and Final, then counter that offer as well. Don't feel bad or guilty about using this tactic; if they want to play hardball, then you also have the right to play hardball.

Like the auto dealers said, the person who gets the best deal is never satisfied with the deal they end up with. They always want more. So even if a Best and Final Offer meets your criteria of a good deal, you should always ask for more, especially with a tough customer.

The idea of using this "nibbling" technique from your side runs counter to the win-win negotiation philosophy. It is counter-collaborative and characterized by some as playing dirty. This may be a legitimate charge from the win-win proponents, but for dealing with difficult negotiators, this is fair game.

If you don't do it, you can pretty much count on them doing it. Tough negotiators don't stop asking for things until they've squeezed out as much as possible in a deal. Getting comfortable with this tactic against any negotiator can incrementally improve deal after deal.

However, be careful about asking for too much in your counter. You can damage or even blow up the entire deal. Getting too greedy can be a problem. I had a CIO of a major networking company, after two weeks of back-and-forth, counter a Best and Final Offer with a guarantee of safety stock for eternity. Needless to say, this sabotaged the entire deal, as the other side thought the request was so unreasonable that the relationship was affected for a number of years.

Here is the appropriate thought process when considering a Best and Final Offer from the other side. First, determine if you are going to take the offer or not. Figure out if the deal on the table makes sense to you; if it does, then accept the offer with one more "little thing." Position it something like this: "We are happy to accept your offer and look forward to working with you on this. Just one little thing we'd like to have and we can close this deal." You want to position that you are taking the deal with just a minor addition.

But if you have already decided the Final Offer is acceptable regardless of whether or not you get your small final concession, if the customer balks then be prepared to pull the additional item off the table and take the original Best and Final Offer as offered. You don't want to jeopardize a deal you think is good or acceptable just to get one more "little thing."

On the other hand, if you decide that the deal on the table doesn't "make sense" to you, that without an additional major concession(s) it just isn't workable, then I would make a full counteroffer with additional concessions from their side. In that situation, you make a complete counter to see if the other side will stay in the game. Who knows, you might be able to hammer out a better agreement if you just keep haggling. And if not, you always have the option to walk away.

Don't underestimate what you can gain by countering a Best and Final Offer. Sometimes, what looks like "just one little thing" ends up being a big deal. I recently worked with a company that is a global supplier of auto parts. We realized in our negotiations that asking for a tiny, .01-percent increase as a counter to their final offer translated into approximately $2.5 million per year. By asking for a .01-percent increase in each of their Best and Final Offers, the company improved their cash position. It was slight, but it was something at least. Getting comfortable with asking for "one more little thing" can take some time, but ends up being a great negotiation tactic.

Why not, when signing the papers at a car dealership, ask them to do a quick oil change or have the car detailed? Neither of these options is particularly expensive for a dealership, but each gives you some incremental value. Why not ask for a restaurant to "comp" dessert for an exceptionally large tab?

I have a unique tactic I use when a restaurant over- or undercooks a meal, or there is some other problem with my meal that is a mistake made by the restaurant kitchen or server and not one I made in ordering (you have to be fair). In this situation some people just go ahead and eat the food as cooked, not wanting to cause a scene. But I see others become rude and demanding, even insulting the server or kitchen workers. I always politely (that is key, as sending back food in a restaurant can have some "hidden" costs if not done tactfully, if you know what I mean) ask if they wouldn't mind providing a meal cooked to the specifications I asked for at the time of my order.

Then I add, "And if you don't mind, because my guests are eating while I am waiting for my meal, could you 'comp' me another glass of wine?" This works almost all the time.

The day I closed on my latest car, I arrived at the dealership to sign the papers and take ownership of my new vehicle. I met with the salesperson and the finance guy in their office with the pile of documents that needed my signature. Not having a pen, I asked the finance person if I could borrow his to sign the documents. He agreed and provided me with his very nice Mont Blanc pen with the automobile manufacturer logo on its side.

I signed all of the documents, with the exception of the final and most important one: the deed transfer from the dealership to me. Looking up I asked, "So, do you get these pens from the company, or do you have to buy them yourselves?"

Looking a bit perplexed, the finance officer said, "Uh, we get them from the manufacturer."

"So they are free to you, right?"

"Yes, that's right." Then he asked with a dawning realization, "So you'd like one of these pens?"

"Actually, I'd like two of these pens," I said.

"And you aren't going to sign that page unless I give you them, right?"

"Actually, I wouldn't say that the pen is a deal-breaker. But it could motivate me to write a good review on Yelp for your dealership."

After glancing sideways to the salesperson, he said, "I think we can do that" and asked the salesperson to fetch them from the front desk.

Now this might seem petty, but in fact the salesperson thought it was a great technique and is most likely now using it on his customers.

Why not, when making a substantial purchase at a retail outlet, ask them to throw in a tie or socks gratis? Why not, when finalizing a deal for a home, ask the real estate agent to give you 1/2 of a percentage point off his or her commission to seal the deal?

You have nothing to lose and at least a small bit to gain. They can always say no. Who knows, you might be surprised by how many say yes."

So how do you know if your opponent is serious about walking away? Consider this next tactic.

#4: Figure out their walk-away option.

Even if the customer knows your product is a commodity and that you need the deal, there are tactics to improve your position.

Sometimes the product or service you sell is a commodity. But even if you are selling a "me too" product or service, don't despair, you still have some leverage. If you already have the business, ask yourself how serious the customer is about giving the business to your competition.

The "big machine" market, like the one my client Caterpillar is in, is very competitive, with the largest competitors being companies like John Deere and Komatsu. Price is always one of the most important factors in deciding which machine to buy, but because the service, support, and replacement parts are so important. And if a large construction company is using mostly all Caterpillar machines (they call them "CAT shops"), they are less likely to switch manufacturers; the switching costs are just too high. Because the replacement parts and post-sales service and support are so important, the cost-per-operating hour is crucial to machine "up-time" and is a major factor in deciding which manufacturer to use. And at least for CAT, a "CAT shop" threatening to convert to a "Komatsu shop" has a low probability; the buyers use the threat of going to a competitor as leverage to get a better price when in fact the chances of them actually changing is quite small.

Just because your product is a commodity does not necessarily mean that the customer is more powerful, especially if you are the incumbent supplier. Before giving concessions, evaluate the "switching costs" the customer would incur by changing from your product to your competitor.

Take your bank for example. Many people are unhappy with their bank, especially these days. But it takes a lot for people to change banks because the "costs" of switching are high relative to putting up with the inconveniences of your current bank. Try to evaluate how "idle" the threat is to go with your competitor before making . . . oops, trading another concession.

When bargaining, good negotiators will pretend they are willing to absorb those costs even if they really don't want to switch. "We'll just give the business to your competitor if you won't give us another 5-percent discount" may be a bluff—or maybe not.

The trick is recognizing an idle threat when you hear one.

Sometimes you can "educate" the other side that the cost of walking away from the negotiation is not in their best interests. It is tough, but can be done.

Elliott Bay is a great bookstore in Seattle. It not only has a great selection, but also has helpful staff, an atmosphere conducive to browsing and, of course, a Seattle-class coffee shop. A couple of years ago, I was browsing the shelves when I came across a book of prints by a famous French impressionist. I instantly thought of an artist friend whose birthday was that same weekend. This would be a great and much appreciated present.

Unfortunately, the book's back cover had a small section that was delaminated. It was barely noticeable, but for a $70 coffee table book I found it unacceptable. So I took it to the service desk and asked if they had another copy, which they didn't. But the clerk said the store could have a new book within a month if I was willing to wait.

Knowing that giving a "promise" of a book to my close friend wouldn't have the same impact, I decided to negotiate.

"Well, I would really like to have this book for a friend's birthday this weekend. Any chance you can get me a copy by Saturday?"

"No, sorry. But we will call you as soon as it comes in."

"Can I ask you something? If I were to buy this book with this delamination, could you discount it?"

The clerk pulled the book off the counter and placed it on the shelf behind the register and snipped, "Sorry, sir. We don't negotiate prices on books."

Like a bass to bait, I rose to the occasion. "Do you mind if I speak with the store manager?"

"He's just going to tell you the same thing. We don't negotiate prices on books. It is what it is."

Not necessarily, I thought.

"That's okay, you've been very helpful, but I'd still like to clarify the store policy on damaged books with the manager."

She went away with a snort and a young man, the store manager I supposed, came and took her place. I showed him the book and explained that, although I wanted to buy this book, it wasn't worth the cover price in its present condition.

"I understand sir, but we just don't negotiate books. When we return them to the distributor, we get full credit."

I had anticipated his response.

"Let me understand something. When you say 'full credit,' you actually mean full credit for the 'cost' of the book, not for the retail price of the book."

"Yes, that's right."

"So I am a businessman and I understand that. But I guess I am having a hard time with the fact that your store is willing to wait a month for a book to be restocked, and then even longer for someone who is looking for this book to come in and buy it, if that happens at all."

"Well, that's our policy."

"I understand. But I am offering to take a damaged book off your hands for a reasonable profit. Your policy doesn't make sense to me as a businessman."

He paused, took a step back, and asked, "Well, how much would you pay me for the book, then?"

To which I smiled and replied, "How much of a discount do you think a book with a delaminated cover is reasonable?"

Get it? And so it goes.

There are also situations in which the customer knows you are in a weak position and you have to deal with that as well. There are similar tactics to address the situation when the customer knows (or suspects) that you are in a weak position and have no walk-away. This may be obvious, but it's important: If they don't know, don't tell them!

A salesperson recently complained to me that his manager sabotaged his negotiation strategy by telling him just before a customer meeting: "Now remember, we have to get this deal. This project is critical to our end-of-year numbers so we can't afford to let this one get away."

The salesperson and I sat down to discuss his sales numbers and he told me, "When my manager says that, he doesn't realize that all the thought and strategy I put into my plan is out the window."

I asked him why.

"Well, if I don't get this sale, my boss is going to kill me."

"Wait," I said. "Does the customer know you have to have this deal?"

"Well, no."

"Then why would you change your strategy if the client doesn't know how badly you need the business?"

"Well, I know I can't walk away. And that's what matters."

No, it isn't!

If your car breaks down on the way to the car dealer, do you tell the dealer? No. Does it change your strategy? No. That would be stupid. If you leave your cell phone in a taxi and figure out a way to acquire another from Craigslist, do you tell the seller? No.

The only time you should alter your strategy is if the other side knows you are desperate. Good negotiators hold their cards as close to the vest as the other side dictates. If the other side doesn't know that you have no walk-away options, don't tell them. And even if the other side confronts you about your limited walk-away, a good negotiator will bluff and pretend there are many options and alternatives.

Even if the customer initially thinks you are in a poor negotiation position, with a bit of bravado and bluffing you may convince him or her that you are in a better position than they think.

I work with a company that is entering new markets with a very differentiated piece of capital equipment, but has a small client base. Every deal and every dollar is crucial to the company in this startup phase.

The most common challenge they hear from potential customers is:

"Well, this product is new and untested so we might be able to do a deal, but we are going to need a significant discount to take a chance like this."

Wrong response: "You're right. Would 25 percent off list price be enough for you to try out our product?"

Another wrong response: "Well, we aren't discounting it that much, but I can give you 5 percent off list."

Better response: "What did you have in mind?"

Best response: "Actually, our company has deliberately targeted you and your company as early adopter. We decided on a select customer base because we want it that way for marketing purposes. The deal we are offering you is our introductory price. Once we have significant market share, which we will, this introductory price will no longer be available."

Now it's their move.

CONCLUSION

Final Thought

This brings us to the endpoint of my negotiation process and to the underlying issue of this book: reconciling win-win with zero-sum. Being collaborative is the central tenet of the win-win negotiation strategy. Being competitive is the central tenet of zero-sum or hardball.

As we've seen, trying to collaborate with someone who plays the "I win only if you lose" game will cost you. On the other hand, playing hardball when the other side is open to a more cooperative approach will damage your long-term interests.

With this book, I've tried to strike a realistic and effective balance between the conflicting approaches; to provide a strategy and tactics for protecting your interests against both hardball and cooperative negotiators, with an emphasis on the tough approach. That doesn't mean you never share your interests with the other side. And it doesn't mean you always avoid win-win approaches. It does mean that until you have a foundation of trust and a good "read" of the other side's intentions, be careful—protect your interests.

If you will indulge me, though, let me share some life wisdom that lends itself to negotiation.

For me, negotiation is a metaphor for life. If you always take your BATNA, if you would rather walk away from a difficult situation than hang in there and try to work it out, then you are out of the game more than you are in the game. And if you always capitulate, if you would rather just get a deal done than negotiate something better for your own side, then you are also not in the game. Life is in the back-and-forth. Negotiation, too, is in the back-and-forth (hopefully, more back than forth after reading this book).

As I teach my daughters, a person can be both tough and sensitive. A person can be both trusting and cautious, thrifty and generous, brave and humble. It doesn't always have to be a choice between one or the other. You just have to develop the ability to read the other side and play all along those continuums. Similarly, you can't take the same approach in every negotiation. Your negotiation stance must vary with each person, situation, and desired outcome.

With this book, you now have many more tools to evaluate the situation in front of you and negotiate accordingly. I wish you the best of luck in holding your ground.

INDEX

ABOUT THE AUTHOR

S teve Reilly consults in the areas of sales, leadership, and negotiation. For the last 20 years he
has worked globally with a who's who of major
corporations. He and his business partner, Steve
Johnson, are the principals for SPJConsulting.com
in Santa Barbara, California. Steve and Steve help
companies in every industry improve their selling,
negotiation, and leadership skills through consulting,
training, and field-sales-coaching. Steve Reilly lives
in Seattle with his two daughters and a dog named
Rocky.

For information on the Negotiating With Tough
Customers Workshop, please go to *www.spjconsult-
ing.com* or call 206.228.9254.